splendored thing

Also by Bia Lowe

Wild Ride

splendored thing

love, roses & other thorny treasures

bia lowe

SEAL PRESS

splendored thing
love, roses, and other thorny treasures

Carroll & Graf Publishers
An Imprint of Avalon Publishing Group Inc.
161 William St., 16th Floor
New York, NY 10038

First Carroll & Graf edition 2002

Grateful acknowledgment is made to the following publications,
in which versions of these essays have appeared:
"Falling" appeared in *The Kenyon Review*, Summer/Fall 2002.
"Lost" was anthologized in *Another City, Writings From Los Angeles*,
David Ulin, editor. City Lights, 2001.
"Seeing Things," "Raptures," and "Apples" appeared in the
webzine *Killing the Buddha*.
"This Mouth" appeared in *The Seneca Review*, 30th Anniversary Issue:
"The Lyric Essay," Spring, 2001.
"Waiting for Blast Off" was anthologized in *Queer 13, Lesbian and Gay Writers
Recall the Seventh Grade*, Cliff Chase, editor.
Rob Weisbach Books, 1998.

Library of Congress Cataloging-in-Publication Data is available.

ISBN: 1-58005-074-3

Interior Design by Paul Paddock

Printed in the United States of America
Distributed by Publishers Group West

Contents

For *Rose,* who showed me what time it was.

It's nature's way of giving, a reason to be living . . .
                              —Paul Francis Webster and Sammy Fain,
                                        Love Is A Many Splendored Thing

. . . it is a high inducement for the individual to ripen, . . . to become world in himself for the sake of another person, it is a great, demanding claim on him, something that chooses him and calls him to vast distances.

                                                            —Rilke,
                                                Letters To a Young Poet

prologue

A disclaimer, of course

$\mathcal{U}$nfortunately, those of us who are cursed with the compulsion to write memoirs have a mighty problem on our hands: the existence of actual people and real events.

The act of writing seeks its own rewards and tidy conclusions. How life truly occurred, often simultaneously dull and labyrinthine, full of improbable coincidence and implausible contradiction, doesn't always read well. In the best of circumstances, the writer struggles for the resonance of truth, a more palatable, sublimated version of fact. (Memoirists often make bad journalists; transgressions of fidelity are counterbalanced, hopefully, by the attempt to remain faithful.)

And it goes without saying that a memoir always poses a bit of a bias problem. The ego of the writer/protagonist demands empathy, sometimes seeks vengeance, and is never above being manipulative. The living reality of other human beings and their authentic human histories tend to get bypassed in the stampede that is the writerly and ego-driven memoir.

We flatter ourselves when we imagine that the ardor of our declaratives will honor those about whom we write. More likely the contrivances and the contortions of our narratives add up to a kind of insult. Other people have their own stories concerning who they are, who they were or might become. Other people are in the business of constructing (though maybe not for publication) their own memoir, and justly feel that their histories and experiences are their sovereign, primary freedoms; it's their beeswax and no one can take it from them. In the end our loved ones might be embarrassed for our disclosures, and wince to find themselves forever linked to us in print.

If we're lucky they're patient with us. They roll their eyes, and go on about the quiet business of living their lives.

In real life our relationships, particularly intimate ones, exist in the safe havens and safe hells we call privacy. How genuine relationships assume their public appearances, unless they exist for exhibitionistic purposes, affect the condition of those privacies, forever changing the texture and flavor of what's possible there, of how we be with each other. Nothing kills pillow talk quicker than the prospect of publication, so it behooves the writer to take a breather, and consider how it might be to preserve the integrity of her relationships.

I have set about to write something for publication about falling in love. This is about me, but also the object of my devotion, a real person whose made-up name is Rose. It also concerns the woman from whom I first learned loving, my mother. Both are characterized as troublesome creatures, but less so because of who they are than the troublesome enterprise that loving can be. This is also about other kinds of falling in love: for a snail, a lion, a boy, a house, a landscape. In so far as these loves have lured me beyond the comforts of the life I once lived in Los Angeles, this book is also something of a travelogue.

I must thank Rose who encouraged me to write about being in love, and who had the extraterrestrial intelligence to insist it had nothing to do with her. Also I owe a great debt to my mother who had the patience to tolerate my obsession with mother-child relations, and who believed with me that there just might emerge a grander disclosure than the details of our very particular lives, in other words, who taught me at a young age that art was a serious inquiry, not just a rant.

For anyone who is in the business of constructing her own story about love, and I take it for granted all of us are, a word of caution: however your loved ones appear in that story has very little to do with who they really are.

splendored thing

this mouth

I don't want the world to be mine (my motorcar, my wife, my house, my gloves, my dog),
I want it to be me *the way my mother's body was before her treachery, and the nipple*
came away in my mouth like a handle in a surprised hand breaks from its satchel, or a
button spits out its cloth.
—William Gass, *The Soul Inside the Sentence*

. . . So please be sweet my chickadee,
and when I kiss you, just say to me,
'It's delightful, it's delicious, it's delectable, it's delirious,
it's dilemma, It's de limit, it's deluxe, it's de-lovely!'
—Cole Porter, *De-lovely*

They say in the beginning was the word, but I ask you, where did the word come from? Wasn't it formed from breath, some proto or pre-proto breath, spelunked through the almighty glottis, and molded finally, given flavor and texture, in the mouth?

The interior's aim is heralded here. Tongue and teeth harness the unintelligible cry. The animal sound is chewed, like leather softening in the mouths of Inuit women. The ensuing speech may define the world; but before vocabulary, the Gods—the gods of hunger and thirst; the gods of thirsts slaked, or of hungers fed, or of cravings denied; the lords of desperation, of need—these Behemoths all roared and chortled from the throne of our mouths.

The mouth is the primal mind. Its first epiphany is the synthesis of gimme and food, its first prayer the utterance of mama. The word "mouth" mirrors the word "mother," matches a summons to a mouthful. These words brim with labial sounds, sounds that bring vibrations to the lips, that coax the lips to open and release their vowels—a e i o u.

* * *

The mouth is the gateway to digestion, to the belly, to the center of our gravity. It is also the threshold to the chest, to the lungs, to our aspiring. The bosom swells in breath and falls in the glory of a voiced expiration, song. The mouth is the I: through its channel we become the ones who are able to receive and who are able to give.

Shrinks tell us that all reciprocity originates here. The I and the Thou appear at the moment our yap engulfs a nipple, at the cleaving of this mouth to that breast. Desire, pleasure, and survival are fused in the form of Mother and in her divine essence, milk. Unfortunately, in due time, she gets tardy with the goods, or tired, or distracted. She's got a self that rears its ugly head, that rises in opposition to this omnipotent mouth, this I and Its Fulfillment, like a rival lover. How can something so beneficent also pose the possibility of neglect and deadly abandonment? How do we have faith in a God who dispenses such sufferings upon the world?

It is our lifelong challenge to tolerate, even celebrate such opposition. The Thou becomes a Jekyll/Hyde. And so does the I. It fragments into a multitude of false selves—complacent, resigned, and manipulative as all get out—alongside that one furtive, authentic holdout, still somehow hungry, still somehow curious. Whatever future cynicism and detachment we feel as grown-ups—however we come to know our limitations as lovers, parents, children, friends—love was always here, first, in this empty, bawling hole.

* * *

Here is a weaning story about a little girl and a little boy. Their world is like their mother's breast: full, generous, without condition. They thrive in the Eden of childhood, before the switcheroo. They are two innocents, as yet unthwarted, as yet unshamed, as yet immune to the world's hazards.

One winter's night, while these children are soundly snug in their beds, their parents sit at the table, their tear-streaked faces lit by a single stubby candle.

"My milk has dried up," the mother cries, "and there is no more bread!"

"There are no more rabbits in the fields, nor fish in the sea, nor potatoes in the ground," cries the father.

It is the time of the famine, and all their neighbors are starving. Some have even taken to eating grass. The parents weep and wail all night. They cannot keep themselves alive, much less feed their sleeping tots. They will die unless they leave this place, unless they abandon their children to the world.

Before dawn the parents set off through the trees, carrying their swaddled and sleeping young. They lay their babies down on the forest floor, in the deepest, darkest heart of the woods. The woman has brought what was left in the larder: a scrap of stale bread, a flask of water. She leaves the pittance there beside them, a pathetic gesture in a desperate time.

Hansel and Gretel wake to find themselves among the damp trees, their rations wrapped in their mother's apron. The last thing they remember of home is her face, so kind as she bends over them in their warm beds, as she smoothes the hair from their foreheads and kisses their lips. Nothing in this world will ever look more beautiful to them than she does. No one will ever be as good. "Sweet dreams," she whispers, sweet dreams."

* * *

A kiss: another's mouth and the hunger for it. The lingual and the labial, the slip and the slide constitute a conversation about hunger. The suckings themselves offer satisfaction, become food. In the interiority of a kiss, our ancient gods of hunger and satisfaction wrestle, they goad one another about the meaning of need. Tongues dart and drag, become bait, lure desire—both to tickle, tantalize, and to sate finally the other's craving, to arrive at the juncture of jeopardy and comfort, longing and rest.

The mouth's interior is soft, silky, supplicant; but the teeth insist they have the power to hurt. Mucosa and tooth play a game of cat and mouse, hide and seek, fright and consolation. The mouth's tools communicate most directly the perils of trust. Oh to be tossed like an infant into thin air, and be caught by the same said hands.

The mouth is often selfish, demanding, infantile. Its job, never forget, is to snatch what it can to sustain itself. It will suck, lap, chew, and devour. It will mew, scream, bite if it must. It can tear flesh, break bone. And with words, it will cut to the quick.

Of course, the mouth also gives. The mouth wants to kiss and make it better. The mouth knew its power at the breast, its ability to satisfy the Other by its own enjoyment. It can ooh and aah, hum lullabies, inspire the resigned, embolden the meek, pray for the forsaken.

* * *

In the mouth we discover our ability to articulate need, to identify loved ones, to call for them, to call them into being and hold them in the mind.

We mold a cry into an appeal, and the mouth becomes an organ of cathexis. We cant and re-cant the name of the Food Giver so that She may appear to us. As language conjures the objects of our most glorious desires, food itself is transmogrified, words become sublimation for what we cannot taste in the present tense. They grant us, instead, the realms of memory, imagination, and projection. The words that issue from our mouths bring us into the world of phantom sensations: hoped-for pleasures, promissory gifts, threats of punishment, the ability to wait. Our young vocabulary, growing exponentially by the minute, becomes our means of anticipating satisfactions that seem ever more remote, of keeping our hungers alive.

In waiting, the mouth learns to savor. It strives to make memory more precise. And in savoring what we taste, in identifying its complexities, we school ourselves in the pursuit of desire, both in the specific, to get it just the way we like it, and in the general, to expand our palates, broaden the scope of our desiring. How do you like your chocolate, milk or bittersweet? Cream in your tea? Salt on your eggs?

We learn to bide our time, to delay gratification. Save the lobster claw for the last bite, followed by a final sip of wine, and always leave room for dessert. Not too fast, dear, or I'll come too soon. Save the best, save it, save it, for last. This is the syntax of our hungers. We are always aware the end is in sight and we want to end it well—with a bang, if possible—and to leave with a good taste in our mouths.

* * *

Our girl and boy set off through the maze of ferns and fir, looking for a way out, but the paths they choose only return them to the same sorry wildwood. Daylight is bleeding away and hunger burns in their bellies, and they stop in their tracks and feast on their meager provisions. Then they have a brilliant idea. They agree not to gobble their bread, instead to leave crumbs of it behind as a way of marking their trail. This would appear to be a remarkable moment, for the children are learning to think, to suspend appetite, to use their resource to its best advantage.

Unfortunately, their scheme is too specialized, their reasoning still swayed by their youth. They assume a kind of ownership of their food, as if no other creatures would dare to eat it, just as they think their mother is theirs alone, with only their best intentions at heart, still baking at the hearth, her breasts full, waiting for their return.

In fact, the fire has been cold all day, the house consigned to cobwebs. She of kind eyes and goodnight kisses is on her way to the city. . . . So long! Birds and mice gleefully trail our lost innocents, gobbling up their markers, leaving the woods as sphinxlike as before.

Days pass and the children are now without a crumb of direction. Their bodies pine for their mother's smells and embraces. Then, as if by magic or from desperation, they spy smoke curling above the trees. It's a house! And not just any house . . . my god, it's a gingerbread Valhalla! Here is architectural alliteration: licorice lattices, butterscotch buttresses, gumdrop gewgaws, moldings of marzipan. Not just hungers to be sated, but all cravings to be fulfilled! A house for the gorging! A home to eat! A return to the womb if ever there was one! "Yum," they scream, and bolt for paradise.

* * *

Mouth pressed lightly to the hand, a peck on the cheek, a graze on the lips—how-do-you-do kisses. Kisses that welcome, some jovial, some dutiful. Kisses with bodies not touching. Kisses that purse the air.

Kisses that are too wet, too curious, unwelcome. Slobbery dog-like kisses. Kisses that are not curious, not dog-like enough. Kisses with the eyes open, kisses with the eyes shut. Kisses that nuzzle and nestle and buss. Kisses that flirt, leaving something unanswered; trifling kisses, and wanton ones. Kisses where the tongue is brave and gallant. Kisses of exploration, of hope. Kisses where tongues roil like underwater mammals. Deep kisses, two bodies pressed into one cave.

Kisses that fall silent and resigned. Frozen kisses that bring on a chill. Kisses that lie, ignore, or withhold. Kisses that ingratiate, kiss up. Kisses with no one home.

Kisses that have appetite, kisses that invite. Kisses that soothe the owie. Kisses that telegraph bliss. Kisses that worship each concavity, each convexity. Routine kisses. The first kiss of the morning, the last at night. Stolen kisses. Kisses on the run, on the sly. Kisses as place holders, IOUs, dancing cards.

Good-bye kisses: some hasty and scatterbrained, others meant to last a lifetime. Letters sealed with a kiss. Kisses blown into the air.

The kiss on the ring. The kiss on the feet, the kiss on the hem of the garment, the kiss on the wall, on the book, on the stone. The kiss that caused a man to drown for love of his own reflection. The kiss of betrayal, revealing a god to his enemies. The kiss of death. The kiss of life, of redemption, of forgiveness. The kiss that woke the sleeping princess, the kiss that turned the toad into a man. The kiss on the cheek of the corpse.

Kiss off. Kiss my ass. Kiss the sky. Kiss your dreams good-bye. Plant one on my kisser. Kiss and tell. Kiss and make up. You may kiss the bride. Kiss me once and kiss me twice and kiss me once again. Kisses sweeter than wine. . . .

* * *

Friction that is wet, that is salubriated with slime, that glissades against the skin is mouthwatering. Saliva is a superb lubricant, and the feeling of slipperiness, of tongue and lips sliding along the flesh, is erotic. Wetness begets itself. Its ability to soften begs for further friction. We rub and rub and it seems that our bodies, like the magic lamps of genies, begin to glisten and shine before our wishes are, at last, granted. With lubrication, the friction of stroking moves from the strata of the skin down to the subcutaneous, to the muscular, and more nerves are audienced, and it seems then that like fish we are able to know our brethren with the whole of our slimy selves.

Saliva with its enzymes, amylase and lipase, breaks down the structure of nutrients into the knowable and digestible. How many infants explore and test objects by mouthing them? How often do we as adult explorers revert to this most intimate knowing? The palate, like a painter's palette, is a way of vivifying the world. How best to know a foreign culture than through the dialects of its food? By tasting one becomes intimate with a culture's ethnic tributaries, its historic relation to invasion, exploration, war, religion, power, wealth, nature.

Saliva is an ocean of organic life. For all its ability to transmit viruses and bacteria—rabies, mononucleosis, and the common cold, for example—it can also act as a salve. Why else are we impelled to lick our wounds and those of those who are flesh of our flesh, our nearest and dearest? The wetness and viscosity of our spit can soothe, it has antibacterial properties and electrolytes that cleanse the wounds, speed the healing process. The same enzymes that begin the process of turning food into sugar, protein, and fatty acids bring on the breakdown of infected matter. The mouth can kiss and make it better.

* * *

I have occasion to be inside this mouth many times a day. Whenever I eat or drink, of course, I bring awareness to that interior place—of the effect a bite of toast, say, will have inside my chops.

There is the initial crunch my incisors make—more of a crinch, really—an announcing sound I associate with toast, and that pleases me like a familiar greeting from a friend. While my tongue rolls the bolus of toast, my saliva moistens it, begins to break it down. Soon it is cud, a blob, a satisfying wad of starch that muzzles the insides of my cheeks. The wetter it gets the more I access its flavor. If toasted just right, the roasted crumb will complicate the starch with an edge of bitterness, give it the depth of malt. I didn't mention the butter and black currant jam, but they're there too, and so is the salt of the butter and the slip of its mouth-feel, the tangs and tannins of the concentrated fruit. It is a lovely irony that the more blended and pulverized these ingredients become, the more distinctive their flavors and textures. The amylase enzymes in my spit continue to deconstruct the starches, and by the time I've swallowed my first bite, the residue in this mouth is nearly pure sugar.

The lexicon of taste has been reduced by scientists and tasters alike to five basic sensations: sweet, sour, salt, bitter, and umami.* Just as its hard to believe that red, yellow, and blue, the primary pigments, could combine with the complexity necessary to describe what we see, it seems incredible that these rudimentary taste

---

*As sugars are sweet, glutamates—a family of amino acids, most concentrated in tomatoes, meat, mushrooms, peas, and parmesan cheese—are umami ("ooo-mommy" . . . really). Umami is a difficult taste to pin down, especially for us westerners. It has been described as "meaty," "savory," "full-flavored," "rounded," and "delicious." Glutamate, like sodium and sugar, is present in most foods, and can stimulate receptivity to other flavors. Monosodium glutamate, MSG, is known for this reason as a flavor enhancer. "Umami stimulates appetites in all cultures all across the board," says Stephen Roper, a professor at the University of Miami. "Indeed, it seems very likely that glutamate drives the appetite for protein, just as the sweet taste drives the appetite for carbohydrates and the salt taste for minerals."

sensations could spawn the palate for all the world's gastronomy, but they do. Five taste receptors, in concert with chemical sensitivity (the astringency of an unripe fruit, for example), and sensations of texture, temperature, smell, sight, and sound—not to mention the elusive effect of a dining companion—are the conduits through which we sample everything from cornflakes to gorgonzola.

Beyond savoring toast, in all its pleasures, I have occasion to be inside this mouth simply for the reassurance it gives me. I do it often, in the same way I silently talk to myself. It is a way of touching base, of half-absently palpating a place of introspection and pleasure. My tongue is always active, always involved in the process of swallowing, of feeling palate, gums, inside of cheeks. I like to bite my lips, to scrape them against my teeth. I like to send the tip of my tongue to search out the fold of skin at its base, the ridge of flesh called a frenulum; or to probe the other frenula hidden on the inside of my lips, especially the lower one. I like to explore the cavities behind my last molars, the craters of gum that once cradled my wisdom teeth. I like, in short, to have some of my awareness inside my own body, particularly inside this familiar interior, friendly old pocket. I have known its dark pleasures for as long as I can remember. It is my way, I suppose, of still sucking my thumb.

* * *

Just think of those two on the roof, in the parlor, at the garden gate! The toffee slates, the cinnamon chimney bricks, doorknobs made of jujubes. . . . To bounce on the marshmallow couch—and bite into it! Think of you and your companion, your animus fondant, immersed in confection, your tongues kneading sweetmeats. Is it not heaven?

And think of that lady, so ambrosial in the starched apron, always cooking up caramel, always planting lollipops in the window boxes! Isn't she something?

* * *

There are also the pleasures and palpations of language, the spoken word, the feel of phonemes on the tongue: Gs gurgling, Ps popping, Ms revving the motor in our maws. In the kinesthesia of speech, consonants are the vertebrae, the clack and click of bone, and vowels are its flesh. Our babble stimulates throat, teeth, and sinus. Language tantalizes our senses sure as food does: sure as sour and sweet, crunch and cream.

Gluttons for repetition, children sing-song their proclamations of love and scorn. They nibble their ditties like candies, their maws stuffed with alliterations and rhymes. They know how repetitions lodge in memory, so they chant their barbed rebukes and ebullient valentines.

Then there's the written word, read in silence yet heard behind the ears, below the throat, phantom mouthfuls, holograms in the imagined mouth. One can practically chew the words as one reads them, roll them over the tongue, gum their textures. We taste our texts in the body's fantasy of speaking them.

Words may not be solid, but for practical purposes (as the physicists say of quantum phenomena), they are physical and substantive. In silenced words, words that are squelched or censored, there is a violence directed toward the self: we hold our own tongues or bite them, we find we must eat our own words or swallow them, they get caught in our throats. We can feel the peril like we feel the onset of the flu. Likewise, we can give someone our word, and that word—like a notary's seal or the word of God—binds us with the solid press of conscience.

An oath, a testament, a pledge, a reprieve. A commandment, a sentencing, a declaration of war. What issues from the mouth can give life or take it away.

* * *

Nothing lasts forever. This gingerbread cottage thatched with spun sugar is about to transform. Our protagonists had envisioned whole days spent just gnawing the walls, chomping the doorknobs, their tongues slathering the window panes. But the old switcheroo is about to happen, as it so often does.

The kindly lady has just coaxed them into a little room, warm and fragrant as fresh-poured fudge. It's a cage, of course, and PS, that lady's no lady. The door to the slammer slams, and it all becomes horrifically clear: They are to be fattened for the slaughter.

From then on the food they're offered looks indigestible, promises are traps, pleasure, bait. No more goodies, or soon they'll be . . . fat as pigs? They are human livestock, tender as veal, succulent as spring lamb. They are no longer at the center of the universe, no longer lords of the oyster, marquises of the dutiful breast. Instead they're edibles, someone else's chow.

Each day the hag checks their body fat. Limbs are measured, bulges probed. And then one day, one bright and brilliant day, they trick our epicurean crone as she adjusts the thermostat in her oven. One big shove and she's a goner. Of course, before ol' Grizzelda roasts like a sauer-braten at 350 degrees, they can't help but notice that she has the same knot of hair, the same bone structure, the same eye color, same teeth, same nose, same . . . well, you name it . . . as their long-lost mother. What is going on here? How can the most good also be the most wicked? How can someone who nursed us try to suck our bones? The sweet house looks sickening now. Besides, they've acquired a yen for more basic fare.

Once you've seen that gingerbread house for what it is, you see that illusion goes hand in hand with suffering. Great expectations are dampened by dog bites, serial killers, excruciating disease . . . need I go on? Mom will turn to monster, sure as sweet turns to sour; sweetie pie turns to bitch, sure as what sustains us lets us down. We live according to two separate and conflicting gospels, one in which we're the sovereign heirs to confection, to the bakery born, each cake scrawled with the goo of our names; and the other in which all delights are, have always been, intended for some other birthday girl, who's never even heard of us. We may well wonder if it's possible to have life and eat it too. Though, by god, that's surely what we're hankering for.

* * *

Curtain up on . . . cake! This one's the wedding variety, three strata, at least, frosted white, draped with ropes of pastry cream, spangled with berries and edible flowers. Two glassy-eyed figurines in formal attire perch resolutely on the topmost tier.

There are times when the beloved is all confection, apple of your eye. Times when she shines albescent as the August moon, pure as the driven snow, bright as a cube of sugar, etcetera, etcetera. She can do no wrong. Then you are having your cake! You are, in the Freudian sense, omniscient and grand, and all's right with your world.

But to eat your cake, to cut a slice with your big sharp knife and take a bite and taste it, is to muss the whole thing up. You mash it in your mouth, make a plug of moist paste, swallow it down, reduce it to fuel. It is drier than you imagined, thin and cloying like sugar water, with an aggravation of freezer burn. OK, maybe it's not like that. Maybe the cake is devil's food, or orange sponge. Maybe it's good, baked by Alice goddamned Waters herself, but it still ain't the icon you covet of Happily-Ever-After.

Because now the worst thing happens: You are full, sated, no longer craving another bite of the damn thing which is no longer beautiful, nor symbolic. There is no pleasure in tasting it, indeed, in desiring it. It has been picked apart. Look at that plate: a smear of cream, someone's hair, a few toppled chunks, a ruin.

So what survives hunger and disillusionment, those two old crones who goad us all our lives? How can we be wise and keep our wanting alive?

* * *

Within this mouth we are schooled in our cravings: how to control them, how to enjoy them. We are also taught, by extension, to recognize the appetites of others, to respect need. And we learn the nutritive value of locution, how to sublimate and attenuate our hankerings, how to seduce the beloved with talk—how, in short, to get, if not what we want, then what we need.

Lips are the inside's emblem, half membrane, a bit of drapery blown out the window, clinging like new paint to the sill. Paint them even redder to signal what can never be spoken, how the body first lived inside this room, pulling milk, translating its poetry, how much of life is still lived in this sanctum, still inarticulate and undisclosed, the flavors of the world washing in like an ocean.

The tongue is a mollusk, polishing the inner walls of the chamber, apprising itself of each texture. Saliva washes over this invertebrate, softening its numberless papillae. Each wriggle and flutter, eager for sensation. It was our initial appendage, the muscle that first wrestled and worshipped the world, and then charmed and conjured its infinite images.

So . . . what if I kiss this place, this wellspring of expression, emblem of the soul, soft twin of your genitalia? In your mouth I taste a brief recollection of our last meal, a smidgen of salinity, the promise of sleep. I drink the sweet brew of your spit, remember milk. Back we tunnel to amniosis and beyond, to be suspended in holy conversation, awash in a sea we can almost taste. The big wide world is all here, all contained in this pie hole that once lip-locked a nipple: the immense void of desire, the spark of curiosity, a capacity both to lie and to speak the truth.

Kissing and biting, lapping and tearing, feeding and being fed; on we go with loving: stuttering, singing, calling out for more. How else to say love, to tell the story, than to bring this mouth to yours?

the real thing

Sara Lee is our *true* mom. That was the line we sing-songed to tease our mother. We chanted how Sara cooked meals for us more often than dear mom did. Though at the time it seemed a delicious way of teasing my mother, it also conspired to rebuke her. Why, after all, should she be required to cook desserts for us from scratch? No flesh and blood mother could really approximate the maternal decathlons of Donna Reed, baking pies, frosting perfect cakes. Besides, my brothers and I knew that what our mother aspired to be was a female Richard Diebenkorn, to spend her days wielding a palette knife, smearing pigment onto large canvases, to come home tired from challenging work, redolent of turpentine.

Not that my mother didn't cook. She made hearty stews and pudding cakes and polenta in a cast-iron skillet. And nobody, but nobody, can hold a candle to her hot fudge sauce. Her breakfasts were positively bountiful: freshly squeezed orange juice, fresh fruit, eggs, toast and jam, coffee or tea. Sometimes as a treat she'd surprise us with pancakes or French toast, then as her energies ebbed, donuts from the local bakery. Finally, when she was spent and resentful, it was coffee cake from Sara Lee . . . our *true* mom.

Nevertheless, her lapses away from domestic drudgery seemed like culinary holidays to me, since Ms. Lee's efforts involved huge quantities of glucose, and, more importantly, because they served up the glamour of the outside world, the gleam of mass production. Each dessert was sealed inside a shining dish of aluminum, and each lid boasted a photograph of a sweet no mortal mother could match . . . pound cake, chocolate cake, German chocolate cake, brownies. . . .

* * *

Of course, in the real world of home kitchens and home culture (with all its pleasures and excruciations) nothing is better than a fresh, home-baked brownie, and poor Ms. Lee's was a wan substitute. The frosting was too homogenized, the cake too industrial flannel. And most importantly, it was missing the wafer-thin crust on the top, that stratum that shone like cooled lava when it was pulled, dark and fragrant, from the oven. The only hit of home-style flavor in Lee's version was the occasional twang of walnut. But no matter, the subtleties of texture and flavor were not its selling points. The virtue of those store-bought brownies was the high, the numbing rush of chocolate and the instantaneous way the jones could be had: from the fridge to your lap, no muss, no fuss. It was a quick refrigerated fix, an accompaniment to a night's sedation in front of the television set, a commercial break, an abbreviated episode of the *Twilight Zone*. And that, precisely, is how I first ate them: after dinner on Saturday nights, cross-legged like an acolyte in front of the television set, my ears tuned to the koan-like axioms that issued from Rod Serling's thin lips.

You had to work the dense cocoa muck in your mouth like a cement mixer, and by the time the last piece had been cut away from the tin and kneaded against the roof of your mouth, you and your tongue were spent. By then, the nerve-wracking theme music started up again, the last survivors on planet earth had learned to love one another, and it was time to either turn the channel or wander off to bed.

* * *

We hounded her for her eventual reliance on convenience foods, rolling our eyes at breakfast in mock scorn, "What, no eggs benedict?"—it was a joke, but since none of us kids cooked, washed or organized the household, those theatrical whinings had a ring of authentic complaint about them, sounding slightly spoiled. What were we thinking? Were we exploiting these tiny transgressions, these abbreviated gestures of maternity because we had felt somewhat deprived of the full measure of her love?

The resentment lardered by a generation of women who sacrificed a career for the mandate of a family, was something few could conceal. As a joke, in her best Jewish Mother imitation, my mother

teased back, "From dawn to dusk . . ." but we recognized in her
faux martyrdom the serrated edge of rage. Our family communi-
cated its resentments in a language of mock disappointment,
shtick borrowed from the vaudeville comics we saw on Ed Sullivan
and Jack Benny, full of shrugs and eye rolling.

* * *

No matter that the mid-century surrogate foods were the gifts of
passive aggression, we gobbled them down. We inhaled those
carbos as if they were laced with drugs (and given the heaps of
sugar, fats, and preservatives they contained, it wasn't a stretch).
But more importantly, we swallowed the high-gloss promise of
sweetness, a retouched depiction of feminine attention. Even the
name *Sara Lee*, had a kind of maternal music to it, resounding with
womanly virtue. So that even now, Ms. Lee's pecan coffee cake
evokes a fantasy—however much I know it to be otherwise—of
wholesome food, indeed, of a wholesome realm at the core of the
American Unconscious. The flavor of toasted pecans, butter, and
sugar—especially with a screech of freezer burn—will always
remind me of Sunday mornings with my mother . . . somewhat
morphed, of course, with that other woman, the woman wearing
an apron, the one in the Norman Rockwell painting, hair in a bun,
cheeks rosy with the heat from the oven.

As far as I was concerned every house across the country was
part of a huge armada, and each had the image of a mother as its
masthead, an aproned Madonna. The goddess had many names:

Betty Crocker, Mrs. Paul, Aunt Jemima, Donna Reed, Harriet Nelson, Betty Anderson. To me, families were tethered, not to each other, not woven into the fabric of a community, but to the centralized mythic family conjured by our TV set, to the comely wraiths invoked by network sponsors. My family was a crude manifestation of the platonic one I saw on *Father Knows Best*.

A collective mirage, a public madness—the residue of which still persists in the current appeal for "family values"—held America in its sway. It professed a righteous life brimming with unconditional love, selfless temperament and godly—not mortal—cleanliness. In those postwar days, the pressure was on for mothers to be larger than life, able to slip the reality of family pain through the eye of a needle, able to become, essentially, someone other than themselves.

And what about the child in those made-up families, the cherub without a care, the one named Penny, Kitten, Bud, Beave? Where could one put one's disappointment in the mortal mom who succumbs to her own emotional wounds, who is tormented by her own narcissistic demands, who wants, as so many women over the past decades did, to be free of the Spic-n-Span glare of the domicile? Where could that child go but further into the *Twilight Zone*, deeper into the tin of intoxicating, if unsatisfying, dessert? Deeper into the retouched fantasy on the lid, the representation of cake, the icon of sweetness? Where was a solution but in the substitute?

* * *

You remember what it was like: "I want my mommy." Perhaps it happened one afternoon when she pulled you from her chest and placed you into the arms of another, or the evening when she waved bye-bye and you were left with the baby-sitter in the wake of the front door closing. . . . You wailed, we all did. We wept so long and hard we forgot who and where we were. We knew only an ancient sorrow, and we knew it was a wellspring, a source never ending.

These days few children are encouraged to transition their need for unconditional love into a faith in the Divine. Yet divine maternalism is continually spotlighted as a means to sell, product. No human mom can match the one confected by mass production, and no religious mom is within our grasp. Where are the tried and true maternal icons—the Marys, the Demeters, the Mahadevis? Where is our four-armed Devi decked out in a starched housedress, all smiles, no distractions, an ample bosom to the tenth power? We are left to a sampling of false goddesses, virtual foods, more sweet cake than we know what to do with; and we are hungry, hungry.

Throughout my teens my mother would complain how my grown-up brothers always felt entitled to raid her refrigerator whenever they'd come home. I vowed never to feel that entitlement, to protect her from the demands of motherhood, to respect her identity as a distinct person, to behave in all ways perfectly weaned.

What home do people envision when they say "you can never go home again"? On what soft-focus set have they staged their place of origin? What gave Childhood its sugary, gilded edge? Even as a child it was clear that no one ever gets the nurturing she craves.

No mortal child ever does. It's a persistent hunger that won't be sated by any meal or caress, but perhaps, someday, by something as huge and as womblike as a theology. Whenever I feel the need for that kind of holding I imagine a place that predates childhood, a place so ancient that no site or word can claim it. The woman who bore me, that distinct creature whose psychology has been one of my lifelong koans, doesn't really exist there. Instead, I am fused with something grander, greater, more good.

"There is no prison so dark and small / as your mother's womb was," writes Rumi, "yet a window opened there,/ from which you saw into the presence."

That, and not my mother's refrigerator, is the place I pine for. O, to fall back into the arms of perfect love, to be fed until there are no empty places. To be full . . . that is, whole.

* * *

Americans, it would seem, are starving to death. Look at the fat ones, struggling to breathe as they struggle to walk as they struggle not to eat what they would die to eat. Or look at the emaciated ones, struggling also not to eat, bingeing then barfing, or simply fasting until their vitals waste. Or look at the ones who yo-yo, who blow up then deflate, also trying their damnedest not to give in to that incorrigible siren, that damnable sin: food. All of us Americans, whatever the morphology, are leery of our own hungers as if hunger might sabotage us from having the dreamed-of body, from finding love, from being whole.

"Why are so many Americans fat?" my Turkish friends ask me at the Universal Studios Tour. These women are neither thin nor fat, just the Turkish version of *zaftig*. We are sitting in a fast-food restaurant, having just trammed our way through the ersatz neighborhoods, the streets where celluloid characters are housed by faux exteriors: to our right, the many colonial houses in which Doris Day frolicked and beamed, comedy after romantic comedy, each time with a different husband. To our left, the European burg, dark haunt to the lurching Frankenstein and the unraveling Mummy. Here's the residence of that nice doctor, Welby, the man who used to be called Anderson, the man who, whatever the alias, always knew best. There's Beaver Cleaver's house, Bachelor Father's, and Jimmy Stewart's when he roomed with that hare.

Fantasy is America's biggest business, our strongest export. We know how to stimulate; we control the horizontal, the vertical, the adrenal. The ride between thrill and sedation has become second nature, occurs at intervals between station breaks, indeed, now every three minutes between music videos. Our bodies keep that kind of time, metering out cravings one after the next. As my foreign friends and I snack at a fast-food restaurant, I notice for the first time, as if my vision had been confined to the fit and the thin, how many people around us are obese . . . one out of every five Americans, according to a recent survey.

Americans like milky things, sweet things, salty things. We like foods with either a pillowy or a crunchy mouth feel. Our threshold for disgust is low. We are paranoid about germs, bacteria, or mold, so we shy from the stinky cheeses, cured meats, fermented sauces. We opt for the bland over the pungent. Our palate seems to have been inspired by a life suckling at a sterile nipple, a life in an incubator. We like our wilderness without brambles, our bodies without hair, our lactose without the stings of complexity. Give us precut slices of Baby Swiss. We want to be coddled, lullabyed, then jolted awake, then put back to sleep.

Food appears at the moment we desire it. Forget hunting or gathering—knowing what part of the animal is chuck or loin, in what field or season the beans came into being—we're ignorant even of the joy of feeding ourselves. Our hunger is not teased (fed, in its way) by our involvement with the process of preparation. We sample no wafting aromas, sips or nibbles; we exercise no imagination in the enrichment of our pleasures (more salt? a squeeze more lemon juice?). In these ways the appreciation of food is merely one of satisfying hunger, or of approximating a recollected meal which persists like a longed-for caress. Eating the exact same meal becomes compulsive, because its repetition requires only familiar satisfactions, quells an anxiety which is never soothed. The pellet appears in the slot the moment we peck the correct button, the same pellet as the one before, as the one before.

Processed foods sound all the appropriate bells and whistles, strike the right poses. Under their spell we become resigned to what Waverly Root calls the "sensation of nourishment," rather than to the real McCoy.

Of course at this juncture, why not cut to the chase and ask what of psychic nourishment? Can we taste the difference between true love and its appearance? Would we recognize the Real Thing if it were placed, hot and juicy, upon our very tongues? Aren't our notions of fulfillment affected by the impersonal ease with which our dinners magically appear? Aren't our feelings of mutual respect dampened by our disregard for flavor, nutritive value, connection to the Earth and its seasons? Doesn't our addiction to gross sensation and fantasy undermine our ability to endure, in fact, enjoy complexity?

What happens to love when we no longer bring curiosity, imagination, effort, even drudgery to the task of feeding ourselves?

This is my first memory: It was knowing that I definitely wanted milk and not water, and definitely knowing they didn't understand that I knew I didn't know enough to make them know what I knew: which was that I definitely did not want water. I knew completely that I wanted milk. So I cried. I heard them say, "She's crying." I heard them ask me again, "Do you want water?" And I thought I had told them so clearly in the same language in which they asked me that no, I really wanted milk. I knew completely then—and sadly—that they did not know my language. I saw that I was not speaking the same language as I was hearing, and that they would never know what I really wanted. I realized then I needed to know more to make them know what I wanted. And I knew that they did not know I understood their language simply because I could not yet speak theirs. And that was sadly something I understood about how much they didn't know. I knew then completely how different we were. And I realized, in every way, how completely different milk is from water, and I cried and cried, and promised myself I would not forget.

* * *

The best meals ignite our imaginations. We are not merely content to say, this is good, but rather, this tastes like. . . . This tastes like a hybrid of peas and spring grass . . . this has a blubbery mouth feel . . . this reminds me of a daube six years ago in Budapest . . . or this smells like apricots. And after you've shared these thoughts, your dinner companion may turn inward for a second, then reemerge, adding excitedly, "Apricots yes, *but with rose water!*"

Then both you and your companion are more intimately bound to the world of apricots and roses, and whatever it was you've swallowed that's held you both in its reverie, as well as, most importantly, each other. You have traveled together down the deep tunnel of sensation and found yourselves mouth to mouth, nose to nose, eye to sparkling eye.

To eat again and again without surprise, curiosity or companionship is to eat without nourishment. To be without nourishment is to be isolated from the source of our food, to have forgotten the smell of the ground cracked open by a hoe, the feel of an offshore breeze, the warmth of salt on your skin. It is a kind of resignation, the hopelessness the amnesiac feels at the unfamiliar smiles of his alleged loved ones. It is the blare of the TV to distract you from your thoughts, the idolatry of celebrity, the glandular jolt that comes with gratuitous, scripted violence. It is Pavlovian and one dimensional, and it will never be satisfying, no matter how many times we peck at the button and are rewarded with the same sad cube of Olestra® chocolate cake. We eat not only to fuel ourselves, but to be nourished by connection.

"So it happens that when I write of hunger," confides MFK Fisher, "I am really writing about love and the hunger for it, and warmth and the love of it and the hunger for it . . . and the warmth and richness and fine reality of hunger satisfied . . . and it is all one."

* * *

My first year away from home I must have gobbled several Sara Lee cheesecakes all by myself, laying down the first few coats of cholesterol in my arteries, giving to myself surrogate maternal pats and pets.

The cherry cheesecake was positively addictive, but only if eaten frozen. Thawed, the cheesecake was merely good; frozen, it gained an edge. It became a semifreddo with guts. Ice crystals made it denser, creamier, slower to dissolve. The sweet cherry topping was a nice foil for all that white frosty glue, the red sugar syrup greased the gears, made the thawing glop slide down into my gullet.

It would be years before I would taste a real live semifreddo, years before I would savor an honest-to-god New York cheesecake or learn to make my own. I am still groping at ways to care for myself, to satisfy my hungers, soothe my terrors; and one thing

I'm learning is to bring imagination to the aid of my digestion, to invite my soul to the table, to feed myself by teasing my pleasures, by being awake.

* * *

The oven is cranked to 325 degrees Fahrenheit and has started to warm up the kitchen. I've got a four-ounce block of chocolate melting in a double boiler with one half cup of butter. At first the two melting fats are discrete. Then the dark blobs of choco-late waddle into the butter like forms in a lava lamp. When the entirety of the chocolate finally relaxes, it becomes the bigger body, and the butter beads in its creases like water on the neck of a seal. Gradually, with a little encouragement from my whisk, the chocolate absorbs the butter, becomes a bit thinner, shinier. I put it aside to cool. By now the kitchen is filled with the husky, complex smell of chocolate. I lick the whisk clean of the mixture and am surprised again by how bitter, nearly chalky, chocolate tastes without any sweetening.

I'm now at the aerobic part of the cooking: four eggs whisked until light. I feel a pinch in the muscles of my forearm as the eggs get brighter, foamy. I pour the equivalent of one teaspoon salt into the palm of my hand and drop it into the eggs (the salt will haunt the brownies, make them indescribably delicious). Add two cups sugar slowly, the granules scraping the side of the bowl. One tea-spoon vanilla, its smell making the back of my tongue heavy.

I swiftly fold in the chocolate mixture, careful not to leaden the airy eggs, then quickly mix in one cup all-purpose flour. A few last go-rounds with the spatula to incorporate the walnuts. Pour the lot into a 9x13 inch buttered pan. Open the oven with its blast of hot air. Bake twenty-five minutes, until the house smells so good I could eat it.

* * *

When I became a child with reason, I saw I had two choices in regard to my mother and to finding satisfaction: to love the woman who does not become a painter, who's maternal embrace betrays resentment; or to support the woman who does what she's dreamed of doing, who leaves the house, but leaves it happy, full of hope. I won't say which mother I got, but you can imagine the odds of a woman of her generation striking out on her own, finding the recognition and fulfillment she craved. Let's just say that woman still has some years left, and damn if she isn't doing her best to find both challenge and companionship as a widowed lady in her eighties. It ain't over, as the saying goes, 'til the fat lady sings. In the meantime, and while I wait for my theology to bake, I have the opportunity to seek nourishment as best as I can, to accept no substitutions, to savor my delights, to say this tastes like, feels like, smells like. . . .

entrance

We must also consider that it is by the entrance of something coming from external objects that we see their shapes and think of them.
—Epicurus, in a letter to Heroditus

Come on, something, come on in
Don't be shy
Meet a guy
Pull up a chair!
The air is humming
And something great is coming . . .
—Stephen Sondheim, *Something's Coming*

et me come straight to the point, the point that rankled me into writing this, the cantankerous sand-in-the-oyster, pebble-in-the-shoe irritant that in time accreted into the mosaic of this text.

It began like this: I was living alone in LA, in the midst of a separation from my partner, and it seemed my prospects for getting back with S. were slim. One morning my friend Alice phoned and said, "You know, Bia, if we're going to find you someone new it would be helpful to know what kind of sex you're into, I mean, are you an *old-fashioned lesbian?*"

The phone went silent on my end while I tried to collect my thoughts. Then the "old" in "old-fashioned" rang like an echo in a sheer rock canyon. Suddenly I had been beamed back to eighth grade, my face chafing with shame, the world's most obvious wallflower, sexual troglodyte, unwanted spinster. And even though Alice is a generation younger, she too had been transported back to my pubescence, a preteen version of her present self, precocious and sexually self-assured. She stood in the crowd of cool girls and whispered and laughed and tossed me looks of derision. In the ringing of all that callow chortle, I rediscovered how it felt to move like Frankenstein, shoulders hunched to ears, face aimed at each crashing footfall.

But then, another image sprang to my defense, an illustration from an anatomy book: an *homunculus,* a human body whose proportions were drawn according to the level of sensitivity. Hands, feet, and face were largest, with lips and tongue nearly filling the top third of the page. Below the face—a great sentient ovoid resembling a radar dish—fingers and thumbs hung like giant gourds from either side of the torso. Toes, like smaller squashes, bulged and sprawled along the ground. Of course the anatomy book, published in the 1950s, didn't even try to depict this sensitive anatomy with genitalia, but I reimagined the figure as female, her sex rising from the narrow stalk of her hips like a small Stetson, its brim including both vagina and anus.

But before we lose ourselves in the lush territory of genitalia, let's linger on those appliances—those fingers, lips, and tongue which just sprung to such enormous sensate proportions—back to those behemoth lovemakers, those articulate pleasers. Yes, it's true, those are the simple implements I bring to bed, the old-fashioned tools of my trade. Should I entertain shame that mouth parts are capable of detecting small traces of nutmeg, trimming cuticle, forming words? That fingers are capable of curing headaches, drawing landscapes, reading Braille? That these modest flesh-bound utensils are themselves eager to be filled up with the pleasures of the Other?

Besides, is the meaning of penetration—the point, if you will—simply to fill or be filled? Are we in the business of moving bulky furniture? Oh all right, I was beginning to feel downright pious as I sought to defend my archaic orientations. And anyway, I do live in the Twentieth Century, I'm not above fantasy, or a snug fit. It was clear I had to forgive both myself and Alice, the *au courant* dildophile.

I hung up the phone, stood in my kitchen, and gaped at the fingers of my right hand. Without thinking, just to be reassured, I slipped the first two into my mouth. I felt my tongue feeling my fingers feeling my tongue feeling my fingers, etcetera—a long hallway of mirroring sympathies, that stretched, it seemed to me, right into infinity.

* * *

For any experience of penetration to occur there has to be a subject and an object, a Self and an Other, an active awareness and an abiding mystery. At some point after our exile from the womb, that paradise in which those distinctions are mute, we've been eager to erase distinctions, eager to push back up the canal and tuck our solitary Selves into a fetal slumber. The cruel joke is that there is no going back, the door is closed. Every Other—rather than promising symbiosis—offers anomie, friction, impossible longing.

Eros is a riddle with no solution. Even masturbation, like the scene in my kitchen, can be a struggle with separation, a confusion of POV. Who is touched, who is touching? In which of those two bodies will my desire be satisfied?

Separation is the spark, the engine, and the destination. Going back to a time before separation, before my distillation into me, well back before my stint as an adolescent monster; back before I could see my parents' shortcomings or imagine their deaths; before I could pester them with the defiance of my resounding "No!"; before I threw my weight toward open space and toddled away from their legs; before I slid through the muscle of my mother's sex and sensed my own way into this world, before then, even, I was separate. It's a fact as distinct as my first breath and all the ones I've breathed since. The distance between subject and object, between hero and wilderness, between lover and beloved, is, will always be, vast.

How do I penetrate? How am I penetrated? Hasn't the wilderness entered the hero, hasn't your gaze already infused my words?

It's no small coincidence that to gain entry to or to be entered is to be entranced, filled with wonder. The workaday garb of the ego falls away, is in fact momentarily forgotten in the thrall of the new entity, in the shock of its presence. Presence: This is the current that links the subject to the object, erases distinctions. Presence demands the essential verb, the primal infinitive. Under its spell we let go ennui, allow the figure to merge a bit with the ground, the church with the state, the I with the Thou.

When I enter my home late at night, move through my rooms without switching on the lights, the house has entered me. Its dark breadth, its still spaciousness, percolate inside me, until I feel safe, expansive within its presence. I claim the dark, or perhaps it claims me. My fingers reach for the wall and the wall reassures.

* * *

Entrances made a splash on the TV shows of my childhood. They were born more of the theater than of film: Loretta Young flying down a spiral staircase, beaming like a summer stock ingenue into the stationary eye of the television camera; or the family of the father who knew best, cast members assembling—again on a staircase—for the audience seated before the proscenium of the TV screen. Another: that talking horse, of course, the famous Mr. Ed, nudging open the stable door with his muzzle and whinnying his "Hello Wiiiiilbur!" with the toss of a forelock. The entrance was an important formality in the weekly ritual of these shows—comforting, affable, ceremonious. Like a good handshake, it had a way of grasping our attention.

But there were creepy TV entrances, too. Talking head Alfred Hitchcock ritualized a kind of droll mesmerism each Friday night, as he gazed from beyond the mount of his double chin, to introduce each psychological drama. Or picture, if you will, a Beckett-noir set—a bare bulb hung above a bleak kitchen table, say, or a chiaroscuro alleyway, newspapers rolling in the wind. Enter Rod Serling, pinched in a too-small dark suit, his upper lip rolled tight as a window shade, an emissary from another dimension of sight and sound and of mind.

The most memorable *Twilight Zone* was the one about the girl who fell into the fourth dimension through a kind of gap in her bedroom wall. Her parents, wakened by her calls of distress, scoured the room in vain. Finally the family retriever blithely leapt through the wall as if through an embankment of reeds, and barked to say he'd found the child but couldn't track his way back. The neighborhood quantum physicist was summoned, and he explained in TV parlance how a tear had occurred in the membrane between dimensions. And, he added— knocking on the portion of the wall where seconds before he had thrust his entire arm—this opening was getting smaller. The father, pressed by the slippage of time, abruptly followed the dog's example and dove through the wall into the unknown.

I saw finally the otherworldliness of the fourth dimension: the swirling diaphanous landscape, like the realms inside a lava lamp. The father's body was impossibly distorted in this alien wilderness, limbs as attenuated as pulled taffy, mouth flared in an Edvard Munch scream. The child was still crying and the dog was still barking, but as if through the drowned and haunted streets of a sunken city. Of course Dad retrieved his daughter before the station break, before the rupture in the space-time continuum scarred over. I was left wondering if that middle-class family would ever again feel cozy inside their postwar home, indeed inside the height, width, and depth of this unstable dimension. Wouldn't the everyday pressure of the ground against their feet give way to awe?

* * *

I was taken with the way she inserted herself into my awareness, the way her face filled the field of my vision, the way she reached for my hand and announced her name. With disarming exuberance S. had leaped through some kind of spatial membrane and filled my gaze with expectancy. She had, quite simply, entered some private part of me and caused me to become awakened, or rather, entranced.

Seven years after S. bounded into my life, she began to disappear. It was as if I could still hear her voice, but the hole in the bedroom wall into the next dimension had sealed itself over; the molecules were no longer pliable, were now shoulder to shoulder, opaque and unyielding as plaster. For twenty months I ran my fingers over the surface of that wall trying to locate some gap into which I might slip my hand, as into the pocket of a coat I hadn't worn in ages, the familiar contents made precious by my longing to rediscover them.

Those treasures were never retrieved. Our cries across the warp of space-time grew faint. We could not find our way back to each other. I could be specific here, give you the details; tell you, for example, the ways in which we had grown in different directions. But trust me, this metaphor has more truth than details ever could. The desire to make love chilled into anxiety and finally hardened into cold resolve. In time, there was only the wall.

In the midst of that estrangement I met a woman at a party. I'll just call her Rose. For superstitious reasons, I can't bring myself to mention her real name, for fear she'll disappear too; and besides, I enjoy the sentimentality the name demands. At that party we talked, joked, sipped our wine, and knew we were each taking pleasure in the other. I wanted to ask her more questions than the party could contain; beyond that and the fascination I felt in her eyes, I could not say. I still saw myself partnered with S., still hoisting the litter of monogamy above our shoulders. I would not contemplate what possibility that new pleasure might hold.

* * *

They searched the valley all morning, hoping to find an opening. The air was hot and muggy and the sawing of cicadas conspired in making them too tired to work into the afternoon. They broke for lunch, and might have abandoned the site if Claude, who had just relieved himself near a stand of chestnut trees, hadn't called the others over to look at a foxhole. Sure enough, when Marie stuck her arm into the hole she felt a cool draft against her fingers. They set about digging out the lair, removing rocks around the opening to what, all three of them were now convinced, was a cave. As they worked their excitement grew; the draft coming from the inside was strong and smelled clean, nearly sterile, an indication that the chamber was large. They'd forgotten completely about lunch. By dusk they'd cleared an opening big enough for Marie's head and shoulders. She entered like a diver, her hands thrust before her, and slid downward several feet before reaching a shelf where she could stand.

Above her, muffled by the wall of rocks, the voices of her companions implored her, was she hurt? She stood up slowly and switched on her helmet light. "My darlings," she cried, "this is the big one! My lamps are being eaten by all the darkness! The chamber must be enormous!" The depth beyond the illumination was as opaque as velvet. Under her lamp the floor of the cave was all confection, a crystalline field in root beer and caramel colors. The tiny needles crackled beneath her feet like brittle ice. She tried to tread lightly, to damage as little as possible. Ten meters before her a stalagmite reached up, its girth the evidence of great age—years in the tens of thousands. She followed its tip and found its corpulent sister pointing down. Then what she saw she could not believe, and she moaned. Behind her, out in the air of the twentieth century, her friends pressed their ears against the opening. Their faraway voices beseeched her, "What? What is it? Tell us!" Up against the stalactite's belly: a woolly mammoth as fresh as anything drawn in Marie's lifetime. She aimed her lamp first left, then right, then in every direction, and started a catalog for her friends that must have sounded like ranting, "Lion . . . bear . . . ibex . . . bull . . . rhino . . . horse, hundreds of horses. . . . "

And even in the following days, even after they returned to the lab in Paris, those creatures roamed across the field of her vision every time she closed her eyes.

* * *

When finally I let myself follow my attraction to Rose, when I both desired her and feared her unfamiliarity, I dreamed that before letting our lips touch we breathed into each other's mouths. The smell and humidity of her exhalations signaled that I had arrived at the threshold of a new country. I wanted to learn its climate, to taste the first word of our new language.

Anyone's body can, I suppose, quickly become familiar, its temperatures, its liquefactions, its goose flesh and racehorse urgencies, its subsequent repose. Physical empathy is hardwired into us. We can learn in an instant how to rub the belly of the dog, kiss the lips of a stranger. But it's the body's inhabitant that causes the frisson. It's that other shore we want to know and be known by, precisely because it is independent from ours, because it can tease, comfort, infuriate, disappoint. Because it has the power to evaporate like a mirage. This is the terror we cannot help but yield to, the wilderness that might just as well spit us out as swallow us whole.

What did it mean when I was, at last, with Rose, one moment of intimacy counterbalanced against the specter of another loss, my fingers finally reaching for her gasp? What possibility did it possibly hold? Or to savor the imprint of Rose's lips as I drove back to my house on the dark freeway? By the hour I scolded myself that nothing lasts forever, yet desire persisted, provoked me like some grail just beyond my reach. Some mystery about her I must know, stroke, chew, lie down and die with. I joke with my friends, but it's no joke: Please, pray for us.

* * *

If you go to look up "penetrate" in the dictionary these days, here at the dawn of the second millennium, and you want a simple definition of the word as it applies to sexual mechanics, you're likely to find something along the lines of "to insert the penis into the vagina of." (To suggest other modalities of intromission—say, to add the phrase "or anus of" or "or mouth of" after vagina, or to substitute the word "fingers" for "penis"—is to understand why the *American Heritage Dictionary* was removed from schools in Washoe County, Nevada for three years solid.) In matters of penetration, *Webster's Third International Dictionary*, the industry standard for American English usage, is dead to the world of fingers, tongue, ears, nostrils, anus, and mouth, which excludes a great many pleasures for us all.

Is it possible that names can codify our imaginations, corral our passions, shorten the fall of our surrender? Perhaps intimacies are better left to the fecund bogs of our inarticulate natures, best expressed with simple gasps and groans. Being nameless, bastardized, our nonreproductive practices have more psychic power, are free to rise from the swamps at night, faceless and squishy, to carry us off in their big strong arms.

* * *

They spend their afternoons among the branches of a tree.

Helen's vocabulary has increased exponentially since she first learned the word, and now her curiosity grabs at every aspect of life, wants to taste and devour. Her teacher still marvels how "water" was the word to stir her, to wake her from numb subsistence. And so they sit among the branches giving themselves to the network of knowledge, held aloft by the vault of that single moment when language appeared inside her like a seed. Since then Ann spills as much as Helen asks for into her palm, as much as she can take, more than Ann thought it possible to give.

Today Helen's father has brought her a dead squirrel to explore. She combs her fingers through its fur, probes every lobe and pocket of its body

*while Ann kneads words into her other hand. On this day alone, while
their fingers roll and tap, they touch upon the class Mammalia, the func-
tion of molars versus incisors, the habits of arboreal creatures, the life
cycle of their very tree. The stroke of Ann's words causes the shape of
Helen's mouth to change, her breathing to still, her thoughts to radiate
new courses of inquiry.*

*And always Helen's fingertips explore her teacher's eyes, her mouth,
or feel for the vibrations in her throat. The child is determined to reach
into the sighted and spoken world. Her fingers taste of sweat, the brine
of her striving.*

*How can Ann ever express her gratitude? Her pupil has caused Ann
to marry her mind with Helen's, to reinhabit her experience, to reenter
the world.*

* * *

The first gift Rose gave me was a copy of *Dreams of Trespass*, Fatema
Mernissi's memoir of her childhood in a harem in Fez, Morocco. It
is a modern story about growing up in a Ninth Century walled city,
where nonbelievers of both sexes mingle in the streets outside the
confines of the harem, and young Arab women forsake tradition
for feminism and western attire. The traditional boundaries
between men and women, between Christians and Muslims,
between old and the new are beginning to disintegrate.

As I moved through the pages of the book, I began to savor its sentences, its guileless childlike voice, its construction of a place that
dripped with exoticism. Wasn't I also standing at the gate, dreaming

of breaching my own defenses, daring to lift my veil? The music of the gift began to saturate my imagination so that each word I read rang with desire. Eventually I had to put the book down. I touched myself then as I wanted her to touch me . . . or as I wanted to touch her. . . .

* * *

There are, suffice to say, as many gloomy entrances as there are grand ones, ones that offer no greeting other than the chill of duty—the kind rescuers must have felt entering the newly splintered caverns inside the bombed-out Federal Building in Oklahoma City, their respirators barely able to filter out the dust of fractured sheet rock. Or the stench of dismemberment.

The second week after the bombing—time enough for the building's bursted innards to qualify for newest logo of devastation—I saw a TV interview with a man who had worked with the search and rescue teams. He had just arrived back in LA with his rescue dog and was met at LAX by the television crews. The mutt at his side displayed none of the usual canine exuberance, only glanced once or twice at the newsman who tried in vain to wrangle her attention. "We've seen some horrible things," the man offered by way of explanation, his voice shaky, under compression. The dog and the man looked into each other's eyes, and saw the same wound. The only solace for the other also dredged up what had been unbearable.

For months Rose and I were trapped in a kind of psychic catastrophe. We fought like mortal enemies. Scratch the *like,* we *were* mortal enemies, wounded by every microscopic slight, ready to strike at any protective reflex. There were insults, threats, exits. She saw something sadistic in me, I saw something mean in her; the more scary we each appeared to be, the more we each snarled and barked. In short, the dogs in us were spooked, and neither of us would extend a hand for fear of having it shredded. We wanted to seal over the entrances with bitterness and never go back. But where could we turn for solace? Our bodies promised refuge from the heartache as sure as heartache.

Nothing I saw in the media during the Oklahoma bombing, not the ruptured honeycomb of the building, not the limp children being rushed away from the site, not the mayor's speech, or even the weeping of the victims' loved ones compared with the devastation wrought on the faces of the rescuer and his dog. They had penetrated the horror and it would not leave so long as each mirrored the other's soul.

* * *

I dive in and my body cuts through. Bubbles of my breath roll up with low scrawling tones. Only seconds ago immersion seemed forbidding, but now its an epiphany for the skin. The water's pressure is everywhere against me, intimate, as familiar as breathing. I feel loved by this frictionless medium. I turn over simply by twisting my weight. I am held.

Naturally, there may be terrors lurking, creatures with rows of serrated teeth. Even the water itself can morph into a monster, pull me under. What first loved me can also eat me, witch in her gingerbread snare, Mama Kali.

Who knows how my life with Rose will go, how this new realm we've leapt into will reveal itself. Will it manifest as a scene in an existential drama, that submerged dimension behind the wall, where forsaken children are crying to be found? Or a walled city, whose veiled inhabitants are safe, yet held captive by the past? Will it be a city of disasters, bombed into rubble? If we are a bit lucky and a great deal brave, we'll advance with our fingers outstretched, allow our fright to percolate inside us. No doubt, there will be disasters, both imagined and real, walls, cries, loss, and debris. Nevertheless, like the dogs who dare, like the famous deaf-mute, like the spelunker, we'll make the leap, because, well, just because we must.

* * *

Come in, friend, through the city gate, the wooden door, the rusty porthole. Climb in, clamor in, squeeze if you must, through the attic window, down the chimney, up the wazoo. Let's unlock, unclench, unveil, make way, lay open, throw open, swing open. Tuck in, set in, slip in, squeeze in, pop in, breeze in, yes, bust in, barge in, thrust in, press in.

He stood before the rocky threshold, hand on hips, and bellowed, "Open Sesame!"

After making the incision, her fingers slid into the abdomen, under the liver and found the spleen.

He could tell, without having to ask, exactly what his friend was thinking.

What he had been saying, she saw now, was that it would never work out, and she saw too, with utter clarity, that he was right.

He woke drenched from the same dream again, the memory of something luminous being shoved up his ass.

They worked three nights solid, without sleeping, until they'd broken the enemy's code.

When stillness permeated the theater, the actor recognized exactly what his performance had accomplished.

 She moaned as she read the last sentence.

The key will turn easily in the lock, the latch clack open, the door creak on its hinges, and you will step inside, remembering everything.

She whispered yes, yes, and so I pushed my fingers deeper, and now I can never, ever forget her.

* * *

But let's not end with a particular couple, any specific pair. What may have rankled me at first involved a conundrum of fingers and flesh, but now it's more than just personal: it's archetypal.

One writes for the omniscient "you," a kind of beloved one wishes to penetrate and be penetrated by. A voice, a guide, a con-science. Someone who keeps us honest, weeds out excess. We trust this *you* as a dog trusts the nerves in his nostrils, as Thoreau trusted his pond, as Sherlock trusted a hunch. Call it the Good Mother. Feel her hand at your elbow.

Then, alas, there is the *you* who finally ends up reading this, a very different creature. Someone who may yawn and scratch her head and skip ahead to get to the good parts. Someone who will misinterpret, indeed who will not listen, who may be callow enough to snicker at wallflowers. Who is, in effect, a wire monkey mother, one who could destroy with indifference, whose milk will not come down. To that entity on that foreign shore, whose language and customs offer no key, no clue, no comfort; O ye of questionable attention span and fickle ways; critic, judge, infidel, dark face of my desiring: to you and all your terrible power, I salute you. Carry me with you, let our adjacent cells mingle, let my words pierce and infect—may they also, as they must, be forgotten, or worse, ignored. Let us endure disappointment in and terror of each other, let the dirt from our gardens cling to the soles of the other's boots, or more precisely, Beloved, let your scent linger on me as mine does on you.

falling

One of the first stories I remember my mother telling me of her childhood was the one about her fall from a two-story window. A hobby horse was thrust up to her, she reached down to grab it, lost her balance and landed on her head. "That's why," she'd conclude, "my left eye is smaller than my right." I'd look up into her face then, not quite able to identify the asymmetry. I suppose my appraisal of her countenance—from infancy onward—always compensated for her facial cockeyedness. Sometimes I like to blame my middle-aged astigmatism on that lifelong habit of correcting the misalignment of her eyes, the faces of everything tweaked and tilted, until now I'm never quite sure if the paintings in my house are straight, the doors plumb, the ground level.

* * *

We are always falling, falling even before our first swaying step. How we could have braved that initial toddle after so many failures, after so many injuries and humiliations is a wonder. Life propels us upward and onward in spite of its many cruel and cautionary lessons. No matter how gravity toys with us, how death stakes its inevitable claim, we skip like the Hamlin rats, drunk with some Dionysian jingle, over the cliff. Down and down we go, round and round we go.

Some people enjoy the sensation. They toy with the threat, scaling the sheer face of a mountain with only a rope and a fly's grip. They dive out of airplanes a mile high, letting their chests pierce the atmosphere. They lash themselves to the masts of kites, falling into currents, trusting the caprice of a wind.

I myself can barely bare any plummet. Roller coasters bully me into thinking I'm dying, airplane turbulence conjures up images of corpses bobbing in the Korean Sea. Put me at the rim of a skyscraper and I'll reel. Even down the shaft of another's eyes and my heart clenches, as if grasping the lip of some imaginary rock, some palpable handle, as if there was one.

* * *

Our first experience of being is one of buoyancy. From mitosis onward our accreting cells can sense the fluid cushion, the embracing placenta, the nourishment that comes unbidden from the steady, pulsing Other. We are born into a state of unconditional love, held, nearly weightless, indistinguishable from paradise. Then, predictably, comes the story of the Fall.

Paradise is lost, the water breaks and we're jettisoned, left to wail and to wait for the return of the Almighty, for sustenance, for a touch. In this sudden desert of weights and sharp edges, nothing lifts us up but the all-too-infrequent appearance of the Beloved, who could drop us as surely as She can ignore our cries. What is there to hold on to but the feebleness of our naked bodies, the accumulation of betrayals, and ultimately, the quandary of faith?

My mantra these days has been "Don't drop me," accompanied by the uncanny sensation of a sprawl from twenty stories. Why? Because I have fallen deeply, indeed madly, in love. Rock climbers and sky divers might welcome the sensation, might find it thrilling rather than an occasion for panic, but I don't. I have confused intimacy with infantile dependency, my new beloved with the Almighty, love with survival. And when I say that I have been thrust into the exact terror with Rose as I had known with my mother—lo, these fifty-mm-something years ago—I do not mean with the octogenarian who lives in San Francisco, nor with the woman who once rocked me, nor with the woman who as a child once fell from a window reaching for a hobby horse. I am talking about the fictional creature who was larger than life, whose mortal asymmetries I corrected with a skewing of my own vision, the entity who was G-O-D.

I know I'm not alone in the primeval terror. A lullaby articulates this ancient mistrust better than I ever could:

Rock a bye baby in the tree top,
When the wind blows the cradle will rock.

When the bough breaks the cradle will fall
and down will come baby, cradle and all.

In any case, the worst thing you can do in a fall—as any athlete, actor, or clown will tell you—is tense up. You fall into a fall, they'll tell you, you trust it, you relax.

* * *

When Buster Keaton was a child, he and his parents worked the vaudeville circuit with Harry Houdini. Legend has it that when the little Keaton took a tumble down a flight of stairs Houdini said, "What a buster!" meaning, what a fall. The moniker stuck, and Buster grew up to be the genius of pratfalls. His brilliance wasn't just that his stunts were daredevil, but that his accompanying expressions were deadpan. As a character he survived his blows with a kind of despairing vacancy. He was, in a sense, immune to a relentless onslaught of misfortunes because he was so accepting of them. Tragedy was part of the landscape, circumstance was to be persevered, and he took his knocks with blank aplomb, his face as flat as his hat. He was called "hole in the donut." "The more serious I took everything . . . the better laughs I got," he said.

Tumbling down stairs, pirouetting on his head like a modern-day break dancer, flopping about in the wind like a tumbleweed, he understood, like any clown, that the basis of comedy is tragedy, understood that a fall on the keister could be a fall, not necessarily from grace, but into grace. You fall into a fall, he'd likely say, you trust it.

* * *

I've been in love before. Not just with the apparition in the nursery. I fell for B. when I was in my midtwenties: love at first sight, or at least first whiff. Though pheromones might have contributed to my sudden attraction for her, consciously at least it was the smell of turpentine that hooked me, my mother's scent when she returned home from painting. B. was as glamorous to me in my twenties as my mother had been in my childhood; she also was a beauty, a painter, a romantic . . . and impossibly remote.

For a host of reasons, most of them youth, our romance was fraught, starstruck, doomed to failure. We saw each other on the sly, when we could, hardly at all. Ah, but you should have seen the letters! Such declarations of love! "I think of you all the time," she'd whisper into my answering machine. We chose one another in part because, like many young people, we enjoyed making promises, though neither of us was ready to make good on them. We made instead a drama of our devotion and loved the sound of our own voices—even after we ended our affair, moved away from one another, embarked on other loves. I offset my fear of falling from her by grasping all the more tightly to fantasy. "I think of you all the time," she'd oblige, three thousand miles away, still whispering into my answering machine.

Years went by, and I should have simply given up the sham, should have realized neither one of us had been brave enough to make it work. I still held onto the mirage of what had been, like clutching an old locket—at the cost, I now see, of subsequent relationships. I'd catch the first breathy incantations of "I think of you all, . . . " and turn down the volume on my answering machine, hoping my old folly wouldn't be found out.

Now twenty years later, if I were to get things right about love, correct my vision, look love square in the eye, not pretty it up, but leave it with all its messes and asymmetries, I'd have to say that promises don't amount to much. The love I touted as the great love of my life wasn't more than a failure, just two people who fell, but weren't there to catch each other, much as they said they wanted to.

* * *

Things that fall are often spilled or shattered. No use crying over spilt milk, the saw-sayers insist, meaning what's done is done, the precious fluid is irretrievable, love is changed. Its the School of Hard Knocks shrug after expulsion from the garden. Once something has been shattered, the damage is complete, unspeakable; someone who is shattered can't simply pick up the pieces, she's broken, done for.

A few things, but not many, bounce. And even the ones that don't, that fall and land intact, like apples say, are left with a bruise. Every day nearly five hundred tons of extraterrestrial objects incinerate before they even hit the ground—their plummet is so dire. Nevertheless, fifty tons of space debris plops through the atmosphere each day with only a charring. Down down down comes the heavenly manna, much of it wafting like dust. The big chunks, the planetoids as large as a house say, wreak the kind of environmental paroxysms that caused an era like the Mesozoic to go poof.

Empires, cities, and stocks fall; as do temperatures, leaves, and the season so named that brings leaves down. Water falls and its submission to gravity continually sculpts the planet.

Men fall from positions of power. Like Humpty Dumpty their empires topple, their crowns upend. Their paths in life suddenly veer into a labyrinth of dead-end directions. We feel empathy for the fallen man. Poor guy, we'll murmur out of the sides of our mouths, perhaps he'll get back on his feet some day. When a woman falls, she falls from virtue, she hits the ground, she doesn't bounce, and no one cares if she gets back on her feet. Guess she got what's coming to her.

Like soufflés, many things that fall have been risen. Up, up; then down. It's the story of our lives: the first half is a great inspiration, our lungs fill, collagen plumps the cells, synovial fluid hoists the bones; the second half and we slowly exhale, lungs deflate, bones grind, cells wither. We fall, in slow motion, out of step, out of touch, out of time, until finally, of course, we topple into the grave.

We have, at least, a notion of a ground upon which to fall, a bottom to hit. A bottom can be a welcome thing, a springboard, a cornerstone, some foundation upon which to make amends. Nothing keeps falling forever, except, I'd imagine, those photons that rush, like lovesick suitors, into the maws of black holes; or some poor soul in Hell, a different sort of Sisyphus, doomed to resist one accelerating downslide, one continual seizure of panic.

Many of us live in the grip of anxiety. Down down down comes that cradle, in one nonstop, vein popping, dive. Why do some experience desperation, while others might fall into joy? ecstasy?

Those first three years are important, but whatever happened to free will? to growing out of the cradle? to getting on with life?

Life wants us to follow a Dionysian jingle, to take a chance, to take up the cup and drink. I should take my cue from the song I quoted as an epigraph to this essay, "I Got a Feeling I'm Falling." I am thinking of Louis Armstrong's recording of it. His trumpet gambols and pirouettes with the anticipation of falling in love. His solo loops and banks, as deft and as playful as any swallow's stunt, soaring at last in one exuberant high C.

* * *

The young, in any species, have higher voices. They tweet and bleat and whinny and wail, and our response is usually one of parental fascination. We think sweet, we think protect. The low tones are generally reserved for the growls and roars of adult combat, meant to signal fight or flight. The scale ascends and we peer over the gates of heaven, the seraphim twittering, the cherubim tittering. Down the scale and our view becomes darker, damper. We see lumbering, hirsute brutes rolling boulders over and over.

Sounds instruct us about our equilibrium and orientation. In microseconds, our brains compare the time it takes each ear to register a sound and, using those two coordinates, map the direction in which the sound originated. We grasp our balance through hearing, and sometimes a dysfunction of the ear can cost us dizziness and a fall. Thus, sounds have their primal, kinetic associations for us. And melody, as it leaps and swirls around us, contains a meaning we interpret with our bodies. There is meaning in the movement between what rises and falls: between, for example, exuberance and despair, between the angelic and the demonic, between the peril at the spire's tip and the refuge at low ground.

And because music is an event in which we rise and fall, in which we are lost and then found, in which we rediscover familiarity after improvisation, in which we touch upon the primeval nerve of trust, it is often a lesson in love. We hold the theme and are held by it. We dip, and drop, and twirl. We fall away, our chests rend the atmosphere. We are free and safe, knowing the theme will catch us like a safety net. Music strokes our earliest kinetic memories, speaks directly to our knowledge of jeopardy, holds us and redeems our faith in being held.

I am thinking now of Cole Porter's "I Get a Kick Out Of You." While the lyric compares the thrill of being in love against the cheap thrills of popular culture, the melody banks like a car on the tracks of a roller coaster. Love is thrilling, the song instructs us, hang on to your hat, scream if you must, enjoy the ride.

* * *

A few years ago my mother, who lives in San Francisco, went downtown during one of the worst windstorms of the century. She was making her way up Post Street to go to her hairdresser. The rain was whipping down and she clutched her umbrella tightly to her body. The gale funneled its way up the city canyon and people stopped in their tracks just to bolster themselves against the blast. My mother didn't think to let go of her umbrella, so a gust picked her up like

Mary Poppins, dropped her a few feet away. She put her hand out to break the fall. Her wrist was shattered in fifteen places. The fracture on her hip was a cleaner break but, because the joint had already been deteriorating, it took months to heal. Already deteriorating. That's the key with older people and their bones and their falls.

She had already been unsteady. Walking and looking with uncertainty at her step. That, in itself, slowed her down, curved her spine, dampened her enjoyment of walking. So, being afraid of falling, she walked less, became more frail, became more prone to falls. She was falling out of step, and it follows that it was only a matter of time before she fell.

That spill cost her. She lost six months of her life in convalescence, but worse, she lost confidence in herself. She was afraid, and I watched her clench against her fear of what might befall her. She is stubborn and vigilant, and god knows, I see myself in her. When I study her face now, I believe I can see her as she really is. I see the smaller eye (though its not as small as she thinks). I see a woman who, like me, is growing older. And I want for her to not be afraid, whatever she falls into in life, now especially, when fear can only make her less flexible.

And I want the same for myself, to let go my grip, change my mantra. When I am in Rose's arms, I have every reason to fall into joy. I remind myself of how life can be altered by something as serendipitous as a wind, of how little time is left. I see myself poised on a rock overlooking a lake. I don't need to be reminded of the thrill of diving into water. I wait for the buoyant notes of Armstrong's trumpet, particularly that sustained, exuberant, high C.

Make me brave, I say to myself, give me a push.

lost

As the sight of land is welcome to men who are swimming towards the shore, when Neptune has wrecked their ship with the fury of his winds and waves; a few alone reach the land, and these, covered with brine, are thankful when they find themselves on firm ground and out of danger—even so was her husband welcome to her as she looked upon him, and she could not tear her two fair arms from about his neck.
—Homer, *The Odyssey*

You'd be so nice, you'd be paradise
To come home to and love.
—Cole Porter, *You'd Be So Nice To Come Home To*

A map can tell me how to find a place I have not seen but often imagined. When I get there, following the map faithfully, the place is not the place of my imagination. Maps, growing ever more real, are much less true.
—Jeanette Winterson, *Sexing the Cherry*

I love maps, and like most people, I throw myself at their mercy when I travel. But it must be said, at the risk of seeming contradictory, that maps lie. Maps of the world are the most bald-faced. They hatch fictions, decorous fibs. Within their counterfeit pages, nations clasp one another as agreeably as hands. Pastel hedgerows softly harmonize. The chaos of ancient rivalries and betrayals, the disorder of homelands seized or surrendered, not to mention blood, human blood, all are masked by a tidy representation of borders—of lines which may be drawn and redrawn, with the steadiest of hands, one year after the next.

Maps of cities conjure a different kind of sham. They claim that the journeyer is not lost; they suggest that life can be serenely viewed from the POV of an angel, that streets and rivers can be surveyed from a loft as remote as a satellite. Maps can't prepare you for what you'll meet head on. There is nothing on a map of Paris, say, to warn the traveler of aromas, kooks, or beautiful women—any multitude of possible distractions likely to divert the traveler from her course.

There are no guides for the city of the nose, the city of the groin, the city of the raised hackles. There is no signboard to warn you that in your travels, that on your journey, whether actual or figurative, you may encounter something that will change your life forever, that will cause you to become lost to yourself. With map in hand you lose a sense that it might, in fact, be advantageous to be lost— to find yourself by way of the city, rather than to find your way within it. You, and every other Joe, wants to know what comes next, what lurks around the corner. And so we consult the guides: the gamut, advice columns, zodiacs, psychologists, talk show pundits.

There are no maps for being in love either; plenty of clichés of course, enough to match our *in sum* weight in archeological detritus. Enough well meaning, but fraudulent, accounts of peas tucked happily-ever-after in the pod—enough treacle about folks trying to cleave unto one another, till death do them part. But I ask you, try to wipe some of the syrup away and what could be less known, more scary? bombs in the night? a plague on your own house? a killer at your bedside? Yes, of course. Then why do my glands respond as though I were being pushed out of a 747? Why the sensation of falling, the plunge into panic?

I've been on dangerous turf before. I've stumbled onto riot scorched boulevards, had shouting matches with crackheads, woken at four in the morning with a knife held to my throat. The avenues, the addicts and the bed are all located in my old neck of the woods, my old turf of Los Angeles. The streets I used to travel across town are infamous for drug deals, gang wars, drive-by shootings. And the freeways I'd use racked up their daily obituaries in the form of grisly car crashes. Like Mr. Magoo I persisted, unfettered, while all around me the dangers of urban life ranted and railed.

I like to think I know danger when I see it, but the fact is I've grown oblivious to much of it, inured to the percussion of gunspray at midnight, the clamor of police helicopters (or even to the sneakier perils, the invisible marauders who ravage the air and rob my cells of their potential years).

Still in the midst of that oblivion I manage to find my terrors. My endocrine system still *sieg heils* to the rigors of "fight or flight." It's just that, like many humans these days, my radar scans and scans the interior. Since I fell in love with Rose—FOR EXAMPLE—I've been animal scared. Why should this be?

* * *

I didn't know much about Ireland until recently. It was just a place on the map, a place that was becoming saturated with cliché, what with all the pop music, Celtic NewAge hype, all the American yuppies swilling stout in ersatz pubs.

But Rose, who loves Ireland, and who has been there countless times, took me there. She had gone there a week before me and was waiting when I arrived at the Dublin airport. We had been together about six months and were falling in love. She threw my bag in the back of the rental car and drove me to a small fishing village. The sea bulged and shown like old green glass. It reminded me, though less green, of childhood haunts in Northern California. We watched the sea in silence, then she drove me to a small thatched cottage nearby. We climbed out of the car, and I knew, with a feeling that gripped my chest and made blood thrum in my ears—was it love? terror? could I tell them apart?—what was coming next. "I just bought it," she said. "It's ours."

How spooky can a cottage be with no attic, no basement, no closets, no darkened recesses? Our cottage (ours, ours!) is about as benign as they come. One story, no steps, floor level with the ground, fireplace in the middle room, sea breeze at the door that never needs to be locked, birds nesting in the thatch. It begs to be lived in. Pretty spooky.

I inferred from the movies that marriage was the end result of love, the achievement, the resolution of doubt. Two people settle in, plumpen, slumber in the cozy buzz of the other's snores. No one told me that love might make me insecure, childish. No one warned me that since Rose and I had fallen deeply and mightily, our pitch into terrors, into fight or flight, would be deep and mighty as well. No one warned me how, being in love, Rose and I would display our fangs to each other in mortal scare.

Let's say you live in a wood. You are a woodsman. You have built your home with the trees you've felled and split with your own ax. There are flowers in the window box, and smoke coils out of the chimney as if drawn with a child's crayon. You know your house and the woods surrounding it, like you know the shapes of your own fingernails, the feel of your tongue inside your mouth.

Then one day you hear an unfamiliar sound echo in the wood. A woman's voice stirs the space between the trees in a way that makes the wood feel strangely reconfigured. Because it beckons, you follow the voice and soon you come upon a beautiful woman in a red cape. At the sight of you the woman drops her basket and flees deeper into the forest. "Please don't go!" you cry. "I won't hurt you!" You pursue her, confident that another look at your affable face, your dependable workman's hands, will reassure her. You cry out to her again, but your voice has become desperate, hoarse. She is swift on her feet and has led you into a part of the woods you've never been. Brambles scrape and snag you. You shred their canes with your nails, wail at the thorns that tear the pads of your feet. Your boots! Where are your boots? And there on the ground, on the damp leaves, her cape spread out like a pool of fresh blood. Whose feet are yours? Whose hands, all covered with fur? Whose strange claws? Whose long tongue curls inside your panting mouth?

And who is the creature who now crouches before you, ready to strike? Who is she?

* * *

In the land of drama, a tragedy ends when the protagonists die; a comedy ends when the protagonists marry. The credits roll, the houselights brighten, people head back to their frozen dinners, known quantities, and insurance policies. But where is the drama that opens with marriage? Where are the scripts and maps outlining its plot? It must be, like the Eleusynian Mysteries or the Eucharist, an esoteric and safely guarded process. Or else it is wholly improvised. Marriage is a drama that ends when the protagonists emerge from the maze, blinking into the sunlight, a drama that ends when the protagonists are found.

Or let's say you are a beautiful woman in a red cape and you are lost in a wood. You come to a house with flowers in the window box and smoke curling out of the chimney. It is everything you've imagined a house should be, and you imagine perhaps it might be your own. Chairs. Porridge. Beds. Let's say you realize this is the house that was promised to you. The house you are to share with your betrothed, a woodsman you recently met while walking in the woods. You are longing for him to return to your house now, for him to hang up his hat and for the two of you to begin the business of happiness. You open the closet to take comfort in the smells and textures of his clothes. But he is there in the dark, waiting, and so are the others.

The monsters storm about the house, claiming to be father, mother, and child. "Who's been sitting in MY chair!?" each demands. It is a tantrum on a grand scale. The baby screams, the father scolds, the mother threatens. Mine. Mine. Mine. Chairs. Porridge. Beds. This is the house of your nightmares that you and your beloved have become lost inside of. There is no place in which to sit and think, nothing to eat, no place to sleep. You could not possibly have wanted this, no.

* * *

Pain is the stuff by which westerners know themselves. Small jabs
of electricity are aimed into the body and the nerves are described
by the routes and velocities through which the resulting pain is
transported. Suffering, like some radioactive isotope, is the substance that is visible to us, that leaves its tracks and maps who we
are. Even animals are judged worthy of humane concern, based on
their ability to be sentient (i.e., their ability to feel pain).

It would seem that pleasure and love go about their business in an
unseen dimension, if at all. I do not want to suggest that pleasure
and love are one and the same, though they do keep company, and
it is true that through pleasure love creates its greatest dangers. Love
and pleasure undo us, working their invisible mischief like worms in
the soil. They aim to corrupt the ego, like Vedic avatars, until we are
no longer ourselves, but more like transparencies that emit more
light, less definition. And that, of course, is cause for panic. Definition is what we crave: lines, shadings, borders.

We are forewarned of the deep, dark, boundless heart. We stand
advised to not venture into territories that are infamous for
trouble. And like good xenophobes, we have begun to reject the
less known, the chaotic. And it stands to reason that, if we are psy-
chologically savvy, we begin to be cynical of love. We want to be in
order, not in love. We want to rise like angels above our bestial passions, to survey our whereabouts, and know where we are. We want
marriage by the guidebook, according to the map.

But then, of course, our maps are always changing. I was advised,
for example, not to kiss Rose until our fifth date; later, to spend at
least one night apart. I've prayed for a satellite's perspective on all our

hissing and scratching and been handed guidelines for "active listening." I've also been advised, only thirty years ago, by people
equally as well-wishing—friends, school counselors, and the
reigning psychological dogma—that love between women is a disorder. DON'T GO THERE!, urge our protectors. They love us; they
see us trembling at the threshold of the maze; they know the interior
is bloody. Why should we risk danger? Don't go.

* * *

A week after our visit to Ireland we were in Istanbul. Our sleep was
furtive, the calls to prayer from a loudspeaker at the nearby
mosque blared, it seemed, incessantly. On our first day we stood
inside that mosque and watched as a hundred or so of the devout
knelt in the direction of Mecca, and prayed.

Later we stood on a hill near the Grand Bazaar and tried to orient
ourselves by a map. We were lost, but the thought of being lost in
such a foreign city was simply unacceptable to me—I had, I
believed, an impeccable sense of direction. As I stood, map in hand,
the vista I claimed to recognize was not the corresponding territory
I saw on the page before me. That is east, I proclaimed, down there
is the Bosphorous. So, down we went to the water, which was not
the Bosphorus. Down we went further and further, the streets more
difficult to descend into. Narrower and narrower, steeper and
steeper. We had not come to the Golden Horn as we wished. I still
insisted that the Bosphorus was just beyond the wall, and Rose,
who had indulged my delusion up until then, had obviously lost

patience. We followed the wall, through a fog of coal smoke, but the ruse was up—I had no idea where we were.

It was rush hour when we finally emerged onto a boulevard. The street suddenly filled with belching cars and busses, and people, hundreds and hundreds. "Look around," said Rose. "Do you notice anything unusual?" As far as the eye could see, we were the only women. All the men were swarthy, many looked like Islamic fundamentalists. Were we in danger? We were lost, we were out of place, we did not belong. I could feel myself starting to unhinge. Would we be harassed? raped? stoned? taken into white slavery?

It is true that the threat of civil war is a palpable sensation in Istanbul, that it hisses and shudders just below the surface. Young men gripping Uzis guard civic buildings. Scores of women show their support for a less secular government by covering their heads in public. The ingredients are incendiary: poverty, fundamentalism, immigration, and a militaristic lid holding down the boil. Nevertheless, despite the burble of civil unrest, despite the hazards of a medieval infrastructure, our biggest threat might have come in the form of an Armenian gigolo, or a Russian pickpocket. Were we in danger? Compared to being a female pedestrian lost in Los Angeles, piece of cake. We were lost, simply, but my reaction carried with it the tremors of greater dangers.

Like Kurtz, I bring my perils with me.

Each time I return to our house in Ireland I check the lock on the door. I worry about the ground movement, as though the San Andreas runs under the hearth. The odd kindness of our neighbors makes me suspicious, and even the birds, who I can't identify without a guidebook, conspire in my disorientation. I am feeling out of my element, turned around, lost at sea, not simply because I've begun to orient myself east—toward Ireland—but because I have embarked on a journey for which there is no compass, other than love.

James Baldwin:

> It is necessary, while in darkness, to know that there is a light somewhere, to know that in oneself, waiting to be found, there is a light. What the light reveals is danger, and what it demands is faith. Pretend, for example, that you were born in Chicago, and have never had the remotest desire to visit Hong Kong, which is only a name on a map for you; pretend that some convulsion, sometimes called accident, throws you into a connection with a man or a woman who lives in Hong Kong; and that you fall in love. Hong Kong will immediately cease to be a name and become the center of your life. And you may never know how many people live in Hong Kong. But you will know that one man or woman lives there without whom you cannot live. And this is how our lives are changed, and this is how we are redeemed.

* * *

Ireland has begun to make her own map inside me. I know the road from the airport, imagine myself driving in the evening light to the cottage. It's almost dark as we pass through the village. We'll pass Flynn's, the pub where last December, Mr. Flynn, of nimble foot and bulging paunch, waltzed me around the dance floor.

We'll stop by Fionna's store for milk and tea. "Were you gone?" she'll ask. We'll talk about her daughter and the weather, children and sunshine, the two Irish obsessions. We'll climb back in the car and drive toward the sea.

I know the cottage will be cold but dry. Rose goes to fetch coal. Then our neighbor, Kate, knocks on the door. When I open it I find her teasing smile. "So," she growls, "she's back now is she!" And looking for Rose: "And where's Herself? Left you to unpack has she?" Her nine-year-old, Eamonn, beams beside her. He is, to condense great matters of the heart into a simple clause, the child I wish I'd had. Kate catches the look that passes between Eamonn and me, and knows it for what it is, and likes what it bodes for the both of us. "Come over later after ye get settled in. Welcome home!"

It's not easy to leave what's familiar. I'd lived for twenty-seven years in the same city, grew up there. I had friends and peers, most of them are gay and childless, writerly and fortyish. Suddenly I feel the gravitational pull of a nine-year-old boy; and of his parents who seem to enjoy the company of two spinster Yanks; and of a bawdy village where an elderly publican teaches me to dance; and of unfamiliar birds who require my naming; and of course, of Rose, who needs me to adventure this with her.

Nothing is certain. How do I proceed?

Let's say you are a hero named Odysseus and you have sailed home to your island. You have come home to your wife, your beloved, to live happily-ever-after. For that reason this tale must be a comedy, and therefore what comes next is yet unwritten.

You have killed the monsters: the wolves, the bears, and the Cyclops. You and wifey know how monsters—if they are true monsters and worthy of their monstrosity—never die, they transform themselves and reappear. A home also continually alters itself, defies maps: one day it's all gingerbread confection, next thing you know a witch is stoking your oven, eyeing you like a pair of clove-studded hams. You are home, at last, but this is just the beginning.

You have only yourselves as guides for what is to come. Bread crumbs. String. Prayers. She slips the red cape from your shoulders, wraps her arms around your neck, licks the brine from your cheek . . . welcome home.

rose is a rose

The rose laughs at my long-looking,
my constant wondering what
a rose means, and who owns
the rose, whatever it means, . . .
—Rumi

Every honey bee, fills with jealousy,
when they see you out with me,
you're confection goodness knows, honeysuckle rose . . .
—Fats Waller, *Honeysucle Rose*

hen Shakespeare compared love to a rose, he must have had a particular rose in mind. He must have imagined, from his seventeenth century perch, a younger variety of *Rosa* than any of the modern blooms found in our neighborhood nurseries. It was an archaic rose, an Alba or a Gallica, the canes of which were as thorny as thistles, the bud flaring into a crinoline dome. It was either red, pink, or white or some mixture in between. Its petals were less starchy than our Hybrid Teas. She bloomed less often, but was more fragrant, more disease resistant.

The rose of the 1600s was not only different in her breeding, but in her conception, her rose-itude. The Elizabethan rose was a full bloomed, buxom flower. Unlike our modern rosebuds, designed for a protracted and less splashy opening, and dispatched by the dozen via telecommunications, she would have been presented to the beloved in the fully opened state, all smell and splay. No pursed bud this, nothing held back. A single blossom could perfume a cottage, and on a humid day in summer, a shrub, in its brief but mighty glory, could intoxicate the garden.

The earliest variety of rose I've ever laid eyes on, or put nostrils to, is the White Rose of York, dating back to the times BC. It is also one of the healthiest-looking plants I know. Her canes are tall and brilliantly bluish green, the flowers white, five petalled, with a forty carat tuft at her navel. She reeks of lime and clove.

She looks old. By this I mean she looks like the original item, the Rose Mother, the kind of posy a child might draw, the flower archetype. She reminds me of the blooms of her distant cousins, the flowers of the apple, the plum, the strawberry, the blackberry— particularly the blackberry—honest, sunny-side-up.

As with all flowers there is centrality to the rose. However petalled and tiered, however labyrinthine, one is always led to the vortex. One always finds oneself like a bee, dozing at the bottom of the cup, rolling drunkenly at its nub. A lover bestows a rose upon her beloved as though offering a grail. The beloved, in turn, peers into the chalice and sees her inner nature. The heart is the essential item here, more voluptuous than a nut, more fragile than a nugget, less rugged than a core, more lasting than marrow, more enduring, we imagine, than the great pumping organ itself. It is an essence, greater than the self that contains it. The rose is akin to the soul, a self at the nucleus of other selves, the fundamental which, given reign, can't help but unfurl, radiate.

* * *

Then there is Rose, the psuedonymous woman, object of this valentine. By any other name, so then, why this? Because she is a flower, and because, as the bard suggests, she resists metaphor. Actively, thornily. Who wouldn't? We all want to be wholly our own, not an ornament in a phrase or a fiction. Not a "character" who advances a plot. How then to talk about the Beloved, without—like the observations of subatomic particles that, it was observed, altered them—altering her? How then for the writer who forages in the heap of personal experience for subject matter, to employ and not to exploit?

She smells sweet, so Rose would, were she not Rose called. So why, again, this pseudonym? Because she raises roses, because her garden and house are always filled with the scent? Yes. Because the rose is emblematic of seduction, of love, of valor, of beauty, of the heart and soul? Yes, yes. Because, being so emblematic, the rose is symbol of symbols, simile personified, metaphor made flesh? Yes, yes, yes. And isn't this the nature of the Beloved, that her essence is made evident in her flesh? that, in a moment of love, she—not the she of her names, nor even the she of her own design—becomes love's emblem, the Divine glimpsed?

* * *

Fossil remains of wild rose plants have been discovered in North America dating back 35 million years, 30 million years before the appearance of the early hominids, our primate forbears, our yet-to-be rosarians. While weasel-sized horses tried to stay downwind of sabre-toothed cats, these roses flourished, seducing the likes of bees and snails. She was, as now, light seeking and delicious, and so was thorned, both for defense and climbability. And she could make of her tangle of briars a safe haven for small birds who'd eagerly relieve her of unwelcome insects.

The first rosarians were the ancient Egyptians. With the invention of irrigation along the Nile five thousand years ago, the Egyptians cultivated gardens, not only for the production of edibles, but for the sheer art of it, for the pleasure and contemplation gardens inspire. Though roses have been raised as a crop, for infusions and for perfume, their primary utility has been to impart a sense of abundance, sensuality, and above all, beauty. Food for the soul.

Two thousand years and over forty dynasties later, Cleopatra doused the sails of her barge with rose water. Up the Nile to the sea, the extravagant queen journeyed to Anthony's Rome, and as her sails filled with the breezes of the river, they exhaled their beguiling scent. ("Purple the sails, and so perfumed," wrote Shakespeare, "that the winds were lovesick with them.")

From Rose's rosebed: Command Performance. Her stem is nearly smooth, the thorns bred into harmless hairs. She's most susceptible to infections of powdery mildew. But no matter, she's like a brood mare, one enormous blossom opens after the other. I pick the oldest flower, the one most like an old floozy, some might say beyond her prime. A few days ago she was mostly apricot, her petals midglide from lemon to tangerine. She has fully opened and what was once orange has begun to separate into streaks of parental pigments, carmine and canary. She smells faintly tangy and—has her color made me so suggestible?—like old orange pulp, sugary and slightly rancid. At her center, which is widely splayed, are five whorls of green. I pull gently at her ninety petals, they tear from her center, like tissues of rice paper. With a magnifying glass my gaze goes right to her fulcrum. Whittled down to her basic organ, she is a hub of his and hers, hairs of boy anthers poised over stickier hairs of girl stigma. The anthers have already surrendered their cache of pollen and their emptied purses darken like old leather. The ganglion of stigma glitter with a stickiness designed to keep the pollen stuck. These tiny cleft heads are unmistakably erotic. I am thinking of other cleavage: vulva, scrotum, glans of the penis, os of the cervix.

Back when the world beyond the Bosphorus was known as Asia Minor and Damascus was its Big Apple, the Persians and their empires knew roses. Their gardens, the hanging one in Babylon included, are legendary. Like Damask steel, like Damask linen, the rose from Asia Minor was bluer, steelier, more lustrous, more textured. Its perfume was exotic, like the myrrh, pepper, and citrus that found their way along the Spice Route.

The Islamics distilled her scent, alchemized her. It takes thirty-two thousand flowers to produce one ounce of her oily extract. Attar, the word we use when describing the essence of the bloom, was also the name of the great Sufi teacher, Fariduddin, aka The Chemist, The Perfumer. It is here that the spirit of the flower and the flower of the spirit are played out in all its archetypal blossoming. And it is from here, with Islam, that our notions of romantic love—the love worth the death of the self—and the rose as its icon, traveled through North Africa, into Spain, to set its roots into the songs of the troubadours and the European psyche.

Double Delight smells like a Bellini, that Venetian cocktail of peach juice and champagne, only the Hollywood remake: peach juice, spicy Chardonnay, dollop of honey, squeeze of lime. Like Command Performance, she's a showgirl rose. A flashy dame with her rouged-up cheeks, her creamy skirts that bleed scarlet at the hemline, her fruity cologne. She just freshened her lipstick and you can almost hear her compact click shut as she turns to give you her best smile.

It wasn't until after the French Revolution that rose breeding took off. A century of global exploration gave new life to botany, and cross-pollination was in full flower. Damasks were *schtupped* with Chinas, Gallicas with Albas, and so on, each successive offspring assigned to an arranged marriage. *Rosa* had her own baby boom, one that hasn't stopped since.

The Tea Rose, like all the accouterments of class-consciousness, was an obsession of the Victorians. Invite a lady to tea: Duchesse de Brebant, Comtesse Riza Du Parc, Madame de Tartas, Mistress

Bosanquet, Mmme Joseph Schwartz. Oh for the aroma of tea imported from the colonies, the intermingling of hybrid pretensions, the thorny social climb. Will you take more sugar?

Reading the names of our twentieth century roses, one can observe how the middle classes in America forged a new aristocracy: Beverly Hills, Rodeo Drive, Polo Club, Lagerfield, Lanvin. In this country, of course, class status is hoist by celebrity, the petard of the nouveau riche, so along with Touch of Class and Class Act we have Show Biz, Razzle Dazzle, Dolly Parton, and Las Vegas. If they haven't already been taken, it's a good bet there'll soon be roses named Spice Girl, Barbara Cartland, Brad Pitt.

Kennedy. The big one, plenty of thorns. Smells of apple, cloves, and vanilla, like a baked apple sitting in a pool of crème anglaise. Wholesome, on the level. In its portraiture pose, the opened bud, there's a hint of pink at the center, just a suggestion of concupiscence, an insinuation of cassis. When dessert is over and the china is cleared, the blossoms slacken in the vase, and their blouses unbutton. What's left of pink is a smattering of burgundy on a linen napkin, a dot of cassis in the clotted cream.

She is a metaphor for the heart & soul of a place. Texas', for example, is yellow. There is one in Spanish Harlem, one that grows on a moonless night, by starlight only. Ireland's is wild and mine.

The women of the westward expansion carried their roses with them. Their visions of a utopian home included a nostalgia for the civilized life, a hope for beauty in an otherwise harsh gamble. They rationed their drinking water to share with their talisman of future abundance. And when they arrived at their bleak destination, they were like the moon walkers, planting their home flags into an inhospitable ground.

At this very moment a bee is at work in the calyx of an Angel Face. The bee moves from stamen to stamen, raking each stem as though pulling grain from a stalk. Its forelegs gather the pollen motes, a harvest that begins to form clumps against its hind legs. At the same time, because its abdomen is bobbing, stray bits of pollen are inadvertently dusted and smeared against the stigma. I can't help but imagine that the rose is actually happy to be engaged by this bee, or perhaps, more accurately, to have engaged it. Her stigma glistens, almost radiant with amber lights. After a minute or so, the bee seems to doze in the concavity of a petal. The rose is all welcome: her scent is honeyed, her petals are pliant, her embrace, tender. This is the dance for which her life has been in training.

From one floral vender alone, three million roses were sent on Valentines Day. Eighty percent were red.

* * *

A rose is the absolute female, the labia like the moist silk of her petals. And so it is with how people like their roses. Those of my mother's generation, heirs of Victorian sensibilities, like their roses in the tulip shape, Platonic, the lips pursed as if for a dry kiss. I'd have to say I've liked my roses fullout open, shamelessly rosy, bodaceous, even veering toward decay. Such differences between generations measure just another inch along the gap: Our roses are like our tastes in music, our etiquette, our politics.

It is possible that one's relation to roses is a kind of Rorschach test. I've wondered, in an analogous Freudian equation, whether those who recoil from oysters are woman shy, or conversely, if those who turn up their noses at glistening kilbasas, peniphobes. Of course this kind of speculation could run into some serious axiomatic silliness like, say, a dislike of fried eggs is really a thinly veiled dread of the Evil Eye. At some point in our psychoanalytic age one must draw the line somewhere—and a cigar is, most of the time, just a cigar—yet . . . with roses? Is a rose just a rose, is a rose?

I like to notice how people smell roses. Some sniff wistfully, their nostrils poised over the chalice from an altitude of an inch or two. Then there's the smellers who lower their shnozz smack dab into her petals. They let their sensors plumb the vortex. They go down. In the process one risks inhaling a few thrips, those tiny rose eaters who look like Lilliputian seals, or coming nose to mandible with a startled bee; but take it from me, it's worth the gamble. What could be better than to feel one's face in her center?

Is rose like a woman in her perfume? In the complexity of a woman's scent, amid seawater, smoke, citrus and grass; amid bread, honey, milk, and scrambled eggs; amid steel and musk is the ever-elusive rose. Though itself a composite and a launching pad for endless associations, the smell of a rose is unmistakable, revelatory. Like the taste of salt or the color red, it is an absolute in our sensory lexicon.

Red ones are given to a blue lady. The red ones sometimes signal carnality, like Rose Red, the schizy double of that goody-goody, Rose White. A red rose is blood, the heart engorged, in thrall, in love, the Holy Cup, the emblem of the heartfelt offering; it also brings the thorn's prick, the gash, the wound, the bloody event that transforms the virgin princess into a conscious queen. A rose is Eros is a rose.

* * *

European fairy tales are rampant with brambles. The thorns that pricked the princess, the briars that enshrouded her castle, the witch's curse, the darker karma that lurks behind every promise, the snag in each pretty deal. Joy is never without the prong, cupid's sting, the wound of love, prick of the prince, teeth in the vagina, serpent's fangs in the apple boughs. Everything worth knowing exacts its price. And good fortune promises outrageous slings and arrows. How could a rose, so emblematic of all that is virtuous and sought after, not also carry its dark briar?

Shakespeare wrote, "Roses have thorns, fountains mud. Clouds and eclipses stain both moon and sun." For all her florid and heady splendor, she is a prickly shrub. Beware as you reach for her bloom. Watch out.

Nearly a decade ago the world was upended by a murder in Los Angeles. *Allegedly,* as we say—until otherwise proven absolute—a spurned husband murdered his estranged wife and her male friend. It had been the emblematic American marriage: two handsome people at the top of the food chain, celebrity status, the self-made climb, the mixing of races, two gorgeous children, a dog. The marriage was both passionate and corrupt, exacerbated by the very icons it seemed to possess: wealth, sexiness, integration, fame. But perhaps more than this, at the core, the mythic pull of the murders was that they dramatized how love could one day turn to rage, how a man who seemed to have everything, who adored his mate, could go berserk and decapitate her.

As if viewing the latest episode of a tragic drama, people from all over the globe watched the televised murder trial in fascination. For the first time in ages—in a world whose attentions had been fragmented by a billion web sites, television stations, zealotries and tribal identities—everyone was held spellbound by a single story: A human being was pushed to his limit and destroyed all he held dear. It could happen to any of us. Shakespeare might have written it.

* * *

Modern cynicism insists that coupling is, stripped of its childbearing imperatives, a serial affair; that lovers are like molted skins, remnants of a particular phase in one's life. Divorce is routine, predictable as flu season. Unions are anticipated with the lowest of expectations. Nevertheless, there is also a prevailing hope, as evidenced in all our popular songs and movies, that love is everlasting, that it somehow survives even the decay of our bodies. Spirit endures, we assert. "You may break, you may shatter the vase if you will, but the scent of the roses will hang round it still," insisted the Irish poet, Thomas Moore. We say of lovers who endure that the bloom is still on the rose.

And when times are good, everything is coming up roses, the warmer weather is upon us, the air is abuzz with a trillion zealous insects. We set the table outside and pour the wine. Later, in leaner days, we'll say we had been altogether too innocent, not vigilant enough. We distorted the world through rose-colored glasses. Our view was delusional, a bit too rosy.

It seems impossible to embrace both joy and disappointment simultaneously. Our inevitable deprivation is a disaster, but what choice was there but to offer our hearts like pretty bouquets?

Rose is the past tense of rise, a rosette, the cut of a gem, a compass card as on a map, a vortex that takes us outward.

We gather them up, smell our moment of heaven, we love the best we know how. So that after the bloom is spent, after the fragrance is forgotten, after the wind has swept the litter of desiccated petals away from the plant, when vines coil like bare wire, when daylight is spare and dusk seems perpetual, the hips burn in the glower, storing their sugars, gleaming like coals.

waiting for blast off

for Jenny, Anne, and Valentina

> *Fly me to the moon and let me play among the stars*
> *Let me know what spring is like on Jupiter and Mars . . .*
> —Bart Howard, *Fly Me To The Moon*

> *If there are species, and rational species, other than man,*
> *are any or all of them, like us, fallen?*
> —C.S. Lewis, *Miracles*

The new uniforms of Upper School were just the tip of the iceberg, a glint of some lurking and sinister peril. Replete with pleated skirts and shaved legs, the transit into high school, into the seventh grade, was an obvious rite of passage, a refinement of girls into ladies. It boded a new and imposing culture, and we lived in fear of making a false move.

Our new sailor-style uniforms probably were intended to side-step the tyranny that might have cowed the less fashion-savvy, particularly the newly immigrated. Yet even the smallest nuance, say the thickness of one's knee socks, separated the cool from the hopelessly maladroit. A plaid barrette was out, a solid in. Two-tone saddle shoes were better than solids, unless they were clean bucks. Midknee skirts meant you were wholesome, an inch higher screamed depravity, but a half-inch lower banished you to geekdom. (The list goes on.)

We were the rookies, learning the ropes, desperate to assimilate. Some of my classmates, like arrivals at Ellis Island, brimmed with hope of fitting in to the new surroundings and making a success of it, but I wasn't one of them. To me, adolescence was alchemy in reverse, gold about to degrade into lead.

There are moments in one's life, lucid, nearly clairvoyant, when one peers into the depth of the future and knows the present moment is doomed, therefore exquisite. Seventh grade was rife with such moments when, gaping into the abyss of high school, I pined for the childhood crumbling beneath my feet.

But this cynicism (or lucidity) was not mine alone. It was part of the zeitgeist. Though Mid-Twentieth Century America wowed us with Simonize optimism, and astronauts were routinely rocketed into space, the apocalypse burbled just beneath the surface. The A-Bomb and all of its sci-fi monsters hulked behind the curtains of every sitcom family room. A new book by a woman named Rachel Carson foretold of a polluted Earth and the extinction of species. The fallout of Freud's bomb continued its contamination of Victorian etiquette among the sexes. And the evil Russians, who promised to bury us and who beat us into space by launching Sputnik, plunged America into an era of foreign espionage and domestic paranoia. Where was progress taking us? The future was a difficult and fearful realm to project into. I should have been able to picture myself like a paper doll: six more years pasted into that sailor getup, then four years in the garb of a coed, followed by a lifetime in a housewife's frock—but I couldn't.

* * *

My pal Jenny was an essential figure of my childhood. From day one Jenny and I were at each other's houses and integrated into each other's family. Her sisters dated my brothers, our houses were only five blocks apart, we went to the same school, in the same grade. She was brainy, introverted, wore glasses and walked on her tiptoes. I was the opposite, preferring the anarchic playground to anything requiring stillness and concentration. In spite of our differences, or perhaps because of them, we were instantly companionable, fastest of friends.

Throughout Lower School the strengths of our personalities melded—she eventually gained confidence in her body, I in my wits. And for a time our closeness was able to withstand even the stresses of Upper School.

On weekends at my parents' country home we'd climb an oak in the late afternoon, hoisting up mason jars, ice, and bottles of Squirt. We'd drape ourselves along the corrugated limbs, talk about the universe and watch the light turn golden, then blue. We'd pretend our Squirts were cocktails as we clinked the ice in our glasses. Later, after dinner, we'd bundle ourselves in our jackets, step out into the autumn night, our necks craning to find Telstar inching across the Milky Way.

Jenny's house was an adventure. It was large, alien and full of old furniture. Jenny had a governess, an old English woman with a creaky girdle named Mrs. Askew. Though our pronunciation of her name was routinely corrected *("ask you")*, we persisted with the inflection we felt best described the workings of her mind.

Sometimes after walking from Upper School, Jenny would invite me over to her house to play her guitar. First stop once there was a visit to her mother who could be found lounging on the chaise in her dressing room tanked to the gills. She had long silver hair, wore mint-green dressing gowns with marabou lapels and cuffs. In her smoky voice she'd amuse us with tales about her last soiree, calling us "darlings" and patting our heads. Soon we'd be itching to reach the refuge of Jenny's bedroom and her guitar, to work on ways to harmonize to "If I Had a Hammer."

Once, at an overnight at Jenny's she slipped into bed with me, suggesting we play "lovers." She rolled on top of me and ground her pubic bone into mine, and I remember being inspired by her sheer persistence if nothing else. Though we both worked diligently at the fantasy of grown-up abandon, neither of us seemed particularly aroused. I was also dimly aware that if she hadn't yet broached this activity with a boy, it wouldn't be long before she did. Jenny was transforming, like her sisters before her, into a beauty.

It seemed we squirmed and rolled together for hours until Mrs. Askew materialized in a wedge of blinding light. Before closing the door and restoring darkness to Jenny's room, Mrs. Askew said only that she was checking to see if we were asleep, but I wasn't entirely convinced. Hadn't she spied Jenny's butt roiling beneath the

covers? Jenny, who had long since stopped caring one iota for anything Mrs. Askew thought, and who, more importantly, had never
had one doubt about her own sexuality, merely sighed and mut-
tered, "So what if she did? Big deal." Jenny sighed again, this time
sleepily, and it was clear our simulation of adult sex was over. We
lay side by side, placid as a pair of shoes. We were, I think, both
grateful to surrender to our sexual disinterest in each other. The
quandary of our pubescent bodies included an absence of chemistry just as surely as it contained passions. "Yeah. Big deal." I
echoed, unconvinced. And so, with our pajama tops knotted up to
our armpits, and our bruised mons of venii, we fell asleep.

What did I fear that might have presented itself to Mrs. Askew's
innermost mind? What in my sphere of prepubescence held me in
thrall, besides the members of my own family? A horse's warm
breath on my palm, the architecture inside a geode, the prospect of
travel in a rocket ship. I was still a child, my libido in a wide, poly-
morphous orbit. The world was my voluptuous oyster. Neither
hetero nor homo, my orientations had not yet emerged from my
universe, like stars culled from cosmic gasses. Nevertheless an anxiety burbled inside me about what I sensed was my anomie. Why
was I different? Why was assimilation so daunting?

This inability to focus, this absence of orientation was not the
perversity that would eventually get me into trouble in Upper
School. It was, rather, my desire to remain a tomboy, my refusal to
forfeit what I considered to be my authentic nature for a feminine
affectation. I wasn't ready to assimilate into the demure world of

womanhood. Perhaps I never would. The currency of tomboyish-ness no longer held any value in this new regime, and would, in a year's time, become a pox.

Gradually Jenny and I saw less of each other at school. Her socks may have been a hair too thick, but her sex appeal and good grades qualified her for the clique of popular girls. I think she couldn't understand why I was so damned stubborn about what I called my "nonconformity." Though we now traveled in distinct and antagonistic circles, we never had scorn for each other. We kept good faith on the other's behalf, just as we had loved our childhood in the trees.

* * *

As the cool girls gravitated toward one another, the creeps, too, coalesced, debris drawn together by increased mass. Anne and I kept company at that time, indignant on the other's behalf, defenders of the downtrodden and dejected.

Sometimes, after school, we'd walk home together and Anne would ask me over to her house. At Anne's the *Playboy* magazines weren't hidden; they were stacked in a pile in an attic bookcase. Once inside the attic, among the squeaky floorboards and her family's collection of odds and ends, Anne closed the door, made a beeline for the bookcase. She threw a pile of *Playboys* onto a small guest bed and then threw herself, as though making a shallow dive, onto the chenille bedspread. Her gesture invited me to do the same. We lay head-to-head, bellies down—oxfords and bobby socks dangling above us—and might have appeared like teenyboppers cooing at photos of their heartthrobs in teen magazines.

Of course we examined the centerfolds with a prurient, if masochistic, fascination. The women in the photos were inhuman, androids from another galaxy, without blemishes, without apparent modesty or shame. Their display of flesh seemed simply receptive, self-involved, singularly devoid of responsiveness. Bodies were as curvilinear and as tan as a pile of Twinkies, the glut of processed flesh highlighted by taffy finger-nails, nipples peaked like meringues, eyes opaque as Necco Wafers, hairdos of spun sugar.

I was not (a big sigh) like the females in those soft-focus photos, and even though my breasts started to swell, I knew I'd never have the kind of body that ballooned and sprawled on the pages of *Playboy*. For one thing I wanted to be a viewer, to touch, to taste, to be the cook, the guest, the gourmet; but not at this table, not among these platters and platters of soft white cake. Anne too seemed caught in a quandary between repulsion and participation, understanding hunger—even as her young body must have—but not sharing the appetite. She must have wondered secretly, as did I, is this loving?

Ultimately though, it was the cartoons that riveted us with their particular brand of sadism. We'd study them and feel the shame of our incomprehension; then struggle to laugh hoarsely, even cru-elly, never to become the joke's brunt ourselves. The ability to find humor in these smarmy gags seemed the key to power—power over the genitals, over lust, over intimacy and identification, and especially, power over the female body. To look at these pages without fear or apprehension was to practice being tough, to study insouciance, dissociation. I concluded I was different, not quite a woman, that perhaps it was I who was not of this Earth. At times I imagined myself to be a case study, the mirrors in my home to be two-way, family members and schoolmates to show a scientific interest in my alien behavior. And I sensed in Anne, my cohort among the outcast, a shared strangeness.

When I was able to fantasize sexually I saw simply a chase. I envisioned myself running through a forest, pursued by an extraterrestrial who's sexual prowess and psychic knowledge of me—once I was wrestled to the ground, if ever—would be like nothing known on earth. Sexual desire at twelve was, simply, anticipation of something unknown, something with which I was not yet able to be entrusted, like a promise to myself from a future me. I put it in a drawer to save for later; I placed it in a time capsule and shot it into the sky. O that I could have made love to the child I was, that I could have soothed her with stories of heroic women, or have showed her a human touch.

*   *   *

Within a year we rookies of Upper School would begin to turn on one another with vigilante fury, to brandish the punishments we each so feared. Deflecting shame, we would become masters at the art of name calling. *Phony, conceited, spaz, lezzy* were just some of the curses we'd sling to keep one another in check. We were learning to recite the mantra of our gender: Don't trust your path, don't stray too far, don't aim too high. This is how, even in that age of rocket ships and astronauts, a glass ceiling congealed to daunt our aspirations.

Queer, inasmuch as it described sexual behavior, was still an abstraction to me, much as any notion of having sex with a boy. During lunch hour at school I'd make my pilgrimage to the Big Dictionary in the school library and look up *intercourse, vagina, penis, homosexual,* hoping a definition might clarify the adult and incomprehensible world. And no matter what I read in that giant tome, and no matter how compulsively I scanned and rescanned it, I was unable to understand human sexuality, least of all my own. I was vexed by the mystery between my legs, by the sphinx I was becoming, by a preternatural creature dashing through a forest, hoping to be pursued by an entity as strange as herself.

* * *

Eventually, of course, I became a homosexual, but not entirely happy-ever-after. Didn't I become my own country, draw my borders and begin to construct the fiction that is my history? Didn't I fabricate an identity out of the cloth of indignation? Of course I'll wear the word *queer*, and I'll wear it resolutely; but O for the seventh grader poised at the exquisite moment, for the child without recourse to a lifetime supply of plot, alibi, just cause. O for the kid and her pal scouring the star-strewn night!

For the uncharted, limitless future! A world, if I might say it plainly, without such strident curfews, without such ruthless boundaries and uniforms.

* * *

In June of the seventh grade I went to my brother's high school graduation ceremony. The young men's voices rose in a solemn rendition of "You'll Never Walk Alone." I imagined walking through a cruel storm, the Valley of the Shadow of Death, a dark labyrinth through which, if one were to lose hope, one could become forever lost. It sounded like a funeral dirge. Walk on, those voices urged, walk on, with hope in your heart . . . I cried, in part for the swelling of the boys' voices, which was a thing of beauty, but also because I could see the approaching thunderheads within the specter of the next school year, and could imagine no end to them. Eighth grade was to be the worst year of my life, and there would be no recourse, no stopping the inevitable.

Within that oncoming squall Kennedy would be gunned down, children in a Sunday school in Alabama would be blown up, and I would begin the small mortifications of adolescence. Childhood was over. What I was trying most to avoid, but what seemed a certainty, would happen: I would be called a *queer*, and I would take that spit wad and redeem myself in the social construction of myself as a lesbian. Of course that victory would be bittersweet. An identity will never describe the protean nature of sexuality, not mine anyway.

By the time I was thirteen I would learn to seal myself off from the abuses of my peers. I would buy a guitar and sing my own songs of alienation and star-crossed love. I would be bolstered by the bookish tasks of latency, the way geeks often are. I'd discover, with the inherent optimism of algebra, how an unknown quantity might find resolution. I'd read how the minstrel cicada first spends its tender years underground. I would read how singing Orpheus carried the imagination through the depths like a torch, until finally he emerged, blinking, only to lose his love in a moment of self-doubt.

But it would be decades before I would learn to rewrite my own bitterness, to hold my head up high and attempt to forgive; decades before I would study the lives of women or deconstruct the psychology of oppression. The century would be nearly over before I would learn that in 1963, the year I tried to navigate a subterranean maze, the year I shrunk from the hope of ever finding my path, while I slipped like an Orpheus into the depths of the eighth grade, a woman cosmonaut, Valentina Tereshkova, orbited the Earth.

This hero must have peered out over the blue arc of her home, far from uniforms, rhetoric, gender, so far even from duty, approval or ego; she must have felt a hunger so pure; must have known what it is to be human, the way the dead know; those who gaze down at our lives, and shake their discarnate heads, and scoff at our time-bound definitions.

like a fish

> *It gives one a feeling of confidence to see nature still busy with experiments, still dynamic, and not through nor satisfied because a Devonian fish managed to end as a two-legged character with a straw hat.*
> —Loren Eisley, *The Snout*

> *Electric eels, I might add, do it . . . though it shocks them I know.*
> *Why ask if shad do it? Waiter, . . . bring me shad roe.*
> —Cole Porter, *Let's Do It*

*L*ike a fish to water, by which we mean, we found our element, what we did came naturally. Water feels like it could be our true medium. At first glance, it seems passive, subject to our desires. We pour it over ice, splash it against our sleepy faces, our wastes whirl away in the pearly vortex. Less directly, it's responsible for the juice in the light-bulb, the food in the fridge. It buoys us up, sustains us. It tickles our fancies too: bubbling, babbling, splishing and splashing. We ski it, surf it, skate it.

On the other hand, it can, as El Niño's havoc insists, transform into a monster. In 1997, the worst hurricane in recent history poured four feet of water over Central America in two days. Homes, stores, roads, whole communities were sheared away by the ensuing flood and slides. Thousands of people were drowned, buried, mangled.

Water, both divine and demonic, is at the root of us. It com-
mandeers our weather, masters our cells. Fluids pour into us;
they slosh, pulse and gurgle; and fluids pour out. We live so long
as we are infused. Infants, we're told, are born with innate swimming ability. We are steeped in a kinetic memory of submersion,
perhaps from those days suspended in the gourd of our mothers,
or tinier still, from our flush cells' cargo of cytoplasm. Even our
DNA bears witness to our stint as fishes, when all our proto selves
dove and wriggled in Devonian waters.

* * *

I've touched a prehistoric fish. I was taken down to a musty room
in the American Museum of Natural History. The ichthyologist
unlocked the door then ushered me toward a crate that could
have harbored a pharaoh's corpse. She pushed open the lid and
flipped a switch that lit the interior. The smell from the tank hit
me first. As though poised over a martini—one that substituted
anchovies for olives—I was instantly loopy, gazing stupidly at a
five-foot fish pickle. The behemoth was submerged in a luminous
bath of ethyl alcohol. The light was yellow and refracted off the
Coelacanth's blue scales and cast our faces in an eerie acid green.
"You can touch its limbs," offered the fish doctor, as she plunged
her arm into the cocktail, and grasped the specimen's nearest hind
leg to demonstrate. The fluid was icy, oily, and stung my fingers. I
grabbed at the cadaver's same hind limb. It felt like the leg of a
chubby toddler.

The Coelacanth evolved 250 million years ago. With her four stubby trotters she was believed to be kin to the mama of all the tetrapods—the Eusthenopteron—the heroic creature who pulled herself, gasping, out of the water and onto the mud, our four-limbed forebear.

Just sixty years ago, one of these extinct fish was yanked up out of the Indian Ocean, out of a distant past, into the now. It was a moment, though less cinematic, like the wrenching anachronism of the dinosaurs in the novel Jurassic Park, a collision of disparate evolutionary epochs: a 250 million-year-old fossil cavorting about in the deep submarine caves off the Cormoros Islands—depths below twentieth century *Homo sapiens* who fished with tools and spoke a language. For sixty years after the discovery of this living relic, fishermen continued to extricate the Coelacanth from the tepid waters off East Africa.

Then a few years ago, and thousands of miles away, a marine biologist from California spotted one while he and his biologist wife were in a fish market in Indonesia on their honeymoon. Somehow, without a current to connect the two colonies, and while centuries transfigured the underwater scenery around them, the species survived, as is, in two separate regions of the globe. Life, within the confines of these regions, never required the Coelacanth to change.

Two mass extinctions have occurred during the fish's oblivious persistence. Whatever grief proved too much for thousands of other marine species—whatever cataclysms snuffed the ammonid, the giant clam, or the razor-toothed ichthyosaurs—it didn't ruffle the silver-blue scales of the Coelacanth. Some animals keep evolving, some die out. Some, like the queer Coelacanth, have the good fortune to stay the same.

Recently I read of bisexual fish, mutations from polluted waters. It was an alarming article, and gave me the same nauseous chill that cheap science fiction films do. Not because hermaphrodites seem freakish to me, but simply because it upset my equilibrium—no "natural" leg to stand on. Our Mother—in fantasy so protective—in reality, holds no loyalty to any of the forms of her creations. Her children are favored in ways we can't anticipate. We are alarmed for ourselves whenever we hear of mutations, it upsets our adherence to forms, by which we really mean our notions of ordered reality, by which we mean it throws us into an alien and discordant time when we—our notions, our theories, our laws, our desires, our bodies— could well be in the spasm of our own extinction. Mutation rears its explicit head in the sci-fi genre: gargantuan lizards devastate the capital city, giant moths batter the sky. What rises serendipitously out of the genetic ooze will someday select us from its menu, medium rare, with a sprinkling of fresh pepper and parsley.

What about our transformations? Can we anticipate which mutation, either in physique or psyche, will present the next opportunity for evolution, the Elijah for a future? Of course we're not likely to set a place at our table for such a creature. We'd sooner institutionalize or surgically correct the geek.

* * *

Rose and I had just finished up our second night's work in our cottage. We set some chairs outside the front door, poured ourselves some wine and seated ourselves to best take in the evening.

"Cows loose!" the neighbor boy offered by way of explanation for racing past us and into our field. We followed excited to see what cows, excited to be part of the frolic. In the midst of our field, knee high in mustard and yarrow, a calf and his mother, both horned, ran wild-eyed while we and our young neighbor tried to herd them back through a hole in the fence. Suddenly the boy's mother made her entrance with a hurling stick, ready to swing at the first bovine threat to her child.

"Hello," she cried, brandishing her stick, "I hate cows . . . don't trust 'em." She stopped to catch her breath. "I'm Kate. And, that," she said cocking her head, "is Eamonn."

She eyed us steadily, and half smiled. She was saucy and tough. Would we take her as we found her?

When I first started living part time in Ireland, I was scared. Would I be liked, accepted? I had been thrown backward in time, and felt marooned once again in adolescent obsession. I was, like my gawky-girl self, other, other, other. A Yank, an urbanite, an outsider, a blow in, . . . a homo. What would the neighbors think? Did I need to claim my identity, like I had in the States, or simply let the natives take me as they found me?

The next evening we went over to chat with Kate as she hung out her wash. Her husband emerged from their house, but didn't join us.

"Now then . . . THIS," she pronounced with a theatrical flourish of her hand, "is my husband, Bill . . . twenty years . . . and still in love . . . ," Then she turned to look at him for the first time and barked menacingly, "isn't that right, DAR-ling?"

Bill leaned against the concrete wall, and exhaled his cigarette. He rolled his eyes and snarled, "Twenty suffrin' years . . . an eternity I'd say." Was he drunk or had twenty years of bitterness weighted his speech to a slur? His fisherman's sweater was frayed and reeked of fish guts.

So these were the neighbors: sour, surly, locked by Catholicism into an abusive marriage. Oh how I feared for the sweet boy who ran so innocently through our grass.

These two people, our neighbors, man and woman, husband and wife, were . . . natural? Undeniably, sperm and egg were necessary for the creation of fish, calves, and children, but not, dear Lord, as a precedent for love. This Irish couple, as grim as the one in American Gothic, was the icon of "normalcy"? Why had I tortured myself with what they, of all people, thought of me?

* * *

For those in the Mollusk family, from garden snail to octopus, gender is the last concern in matters of sex. Who wears the top hat and who wears the teddy are of no consequence. Squids and periwinkles, for example, negotiate who will lead and who will follow long after the dance is underway. How the consensus concerning these matters is arrived at, no one knows. But from that moment on, the behaviors of complementary genders are in swing. One critter will be penetrated; the other will penetrate.

Female seagulls sometimes shack up, have a kind of Boston Marriage. So do female vampire bats. Bonobos, our closest genetic relatives, are as pansexual as the day is long. Which is all to say that nature's ways are bisexual both in gender and in sexual practice.

Then there's all the many baubles in nature's cornucopia that weren't selected "naturally," that are actually born of human design. Look at the cultivation of roses, their lineage, like the oldest, and most incestuous of royal families, nature pulled through the sieve of culture, distilled for beauty's sake, honey for our human hive. We have surrounded ourselves, gated ourselves, in a rococo garden, trampled or weeded out the less desirable species, cultivated and hybridized the life forms that most please us. Would the horse be with us, ill fitted as she is for evolution, were it not for the aesthetics of our desire? Would the dairy cow, the boysenberry, the tea rose?

Why then do we look to nature as the standard bearer, as though we were teenagers eager to disregard our mother, yet craving her guidance all the while? As if nature contained something as petty as a point of view to instruct us. To ask, as we must, what is natural, by which we mean, who are we? who do we want to become? Sex brings us to the altar of nature, forces us to genuflect to its genital power, but how exactly we practice our natures, how we worship, is a flourish only we can choreograph.

We think, for example, kissing is as natural an expression as, say, crying; yet this practice, like others, can present a challenge when trying to separate custom from reflex. Shocking as it may be to us westerners, kissing lips to lips, mouth upon slippery mouth, is as decidedly unerotic to other sexually-active people as licking a sidewalk. For some, olfactory kisses, nose to nuzzling nose, breath upon the beloved's breath, is the sexy item.

The first time I had sex with a man I felt like I took to it like a fish to water. Then, to my delight, with a woman, also like a fish to water. Both were "natural," I knew what to do. And yet I was also learning. Learning not only the gestural language of sex: its verbs and nouns, the virtues of simple verses complex sentences, the variety of its prepositional phrases (up, down, in, around, out and over, et al); but also learning about sexual sensation, learning like a baby, to know myself by an ability to identify and articulate feeling. Which is to say, again, that these waters, which appear about as natural as tears, are actually socially constructed—but not unnatural.

* * *

Fishes see and hear of course, but also have smell receptors everywhere on their bodies. Pheremones from here and there alert them to both predators and suitors. And, as they preambulate in the water, their undulations generate currents their fellow fish can feel.

While our sense organs have evolved to become specialized, primarily in the tangle of nerves from eye to cortex to fingers, fish are more like sensory generalists, jacks-of-all-trades. Their receptivity includes even an electromagnetic sense. What must it be like to experience the environment as it registers on our skin, through pressure, texture, movement, and temperature? What is it like to feel the electron charge of hundreds of your brethren as they carousel in unison with you?

One remembers in sex what it is to be a fish, to move in the liquid environment, to become all sensation again, to imagine oneself—however much a conceit—as electromagnetically sensitive.

Inside our bodies is the sea of our blood, the water of our flesh, the cellular lives within the one life. The interior brew, intricate and miraculous in its physiology, is equally so in its personhood. We each house a life of dreams, of submersion, of great longings and conviction. And like the life in an ocean, we are teaming with monsters, protean creatures, Goliaths. And Love can slake your thirst, or smash your world as hard as any hurricane or tsunami.

* * *

One night I sat next to our neighbor Bill at the village pub. There was a song contest on and Kate was waiting in line to step up on the small platform to the mic. "I love to see her sing," he whispered to me, as if he were confessing his continual bafflement with one of life's most profound mysteries. With a voice and delivery of a fifteen-year-old, Kate crooned a version of "Endless Love"—nothing like the bellow I'd heard calling her son to supper, nor the growl that scolded Bill at the front door. Occasionally she'd glance at Bill and a smile would flicker. I turned to catch his response. He faced me and showed me his tears. I was shocked. Did they actually love each other?

After the song was over, Kate gave up the mic to the next contestant and squeezed herself on the bench between Bill and me. He

pretended to grab her ass as she sat. "Go fuck yourself!" she com-
manded. "It's been so long, I'd say that's a good idea," he snarled,
exhaling cigarette smoke. Kate pretended to ignore him, so he
shook his fist at the back of her head, the mock threat Ralph
Kramden would have used to accompany his "To the moon, Alice
. . . to the moon!" This was their schtick, part of their play. The
affection between them was palpable.

Where I came from, end-of-the-millennium gay Los Angeles, the
average life expectancy of a union is three to seven years. In that culture
of psycho-therapies and self-help literatures, theories abound about
the causes for these brief partnerships: modern individuals, newly lib-
erated from the claims of childrearing, are free to seek consecutive,
serial partnerships, free to change, free to seek self-fulfillment, free to
pursue a realization of self, of being—first and foremost—an individual in perpetual pursuit of individuation. Where I came from most
everyone I knew was in therapy. Where I came from you'd sooner tell
your therapist or friends your deepest feelings than your spouse, you'd
sooner wed yourself, your friends, or your work than your partner.
Nothing wrong with that, after all they're more durable than your
lover by a long shot. Where I came from. . . .

"Do you two fight?" I ask Kate.

"Well, I'd say so, but we never go to bed mad. Now, I'd say even
if I know I'm right, I'd apologize . . . because it's the making up
that's sooo nice. . . . But then, say at five in the morning, . . . I might
be right again! And we're off!"

"We never have a row in public. It's between us. We would never
embarrass each other in front of anyone else. We don't air our

problems with others. It's just respect. Now, at home . . . we throw the china."

"What do the kids do when the china is flying?" I ask, frightened by the fierce side of love, the storm in myself.

"Duck!"

I've never said anything explicit to our neighbors about my relationship with Rose. I'm not sure how "lesbian" would go down, though I'm certain it would glare, like the blowhards they watch on the daytime talk shows via satellite, of the American rage for identity. Besides, they know, perhaps better than my sophisticated friends back in California, what our relationship is.

One night Kate and Bill and Rose and I stood in our attached outbuilding, which had once been the old milking barn. Rose and I had made sketches on paper and drawn chalk lines on the walls to plan the conversion of this structure into our second bedroom.

When she saw the layout, Kate piped up, "Ah, so when the two of you have a row, Bia—you can come over here. Right?" She laughed, and I replied with a "Right!" Enough was said, and more. Bill gave me a sweet smile, then rolled his eyes at me the way Ralph Kramden did to Ed Norton.

* * *

After touching the old fish at the Museum of Natural History my fingers stunk for hours. I washed them with soap, I washed them with vinegar, I rubbed them with a quartered lemon. It was a smell that seemed distilled by centuries of prehuman survival. There had been something grotesque about a creature that old, that outdated. And that unpleasantness was, simply, a close encounter with Cosmic Disregard. Nature's immensity made a mockery of my life-time concerns: motes as transient and as petty as homophobia, and its bastard child-mote, "gay identity."

There is nothing conclusively natural concerning human bonding—except that humans bond conclusively. That is the only smell that will not wash off. The Welsh writer Jan Morris said it well, as she contemplated the spawning of trout in a river near her home, " . . . thinking of them with admiration, though I can not see them, I realize that nature's first message . . . is that love is strenuous and risky, comes in all kinds, and moves mysteriously."

* * *

Last September, Eamonn took us fishing for mackerel. He rallied his parents, then rallied us. The five of us walked through the fields to the cliffs overlooking the Irish Sea. The water spread calmly until it blended with the horizon.

We gazed down the coastline at the shale cliffs: the strata of old sea floors, now dipping and vaulting, folded like bolts of heavy felt. People had been climbing down to the rocks below us for centuries, angling at the end of summer for the same silver fish. We scrambled down to the water through tufts of dwarf gorse and heather.

The sea was gentle after the weekend's storm. It lapped at my boots while seals lifted their heads and eyed us. Cormorants slipped under the pewter surface, then reappeared a moment later. What else was down there under that dark skirt? I thought of my literary forebear, Loren Eisley, "There are other things brewing and growing in the oceanic vat. It pays to know this. It pays to know there is just as much future as there is past. The only thing that doesn't pay is to be sure of man's own part in it."

Bill ran, as surefooted as a mountain goat, between Eamonn and me, untangling snarled lines, and showing us, one more time, how to cast out. In minutes we were hauling up fish. Eamonn shot me one worried look, to see if I was managing my pole, then returned, gleeful, to focus on himself. He squealed with each catch. We flung back our trophies to Rose and Kate, who had busied themselves with the macabre—and from the sound of it—hilarious business of murder. "Die, you fucker!" Kate cried as she broke each mackerel vertebrae. Bill smoked awhile and looked at the sea, then fished awhile with my pole. We reeled in thirty fish before we decided, much to Eamonn's dismay, that the light was too dim and the air too chill.

We were an odd little group of humans: Bill, Kate, and Eamonn, odd and out of place in their way for cherishing their surroundings as if they, too, were blow ins. Rose and me, the urbane spinsters, so cautious to tread the spines of sea-worn shale.

"Now ye know about this place," instructed our Kate. "Ye can come down here, anytime, you know, . . . if you're having a row or you need to just get away and think."

We all ambled up the rocks, then up the grassy cliffs, across the fields to home. We carried our lucre from the sea, soaked with brine and guts and blood, plunged together, inexplicable friends.

seeing things

I would like to step out of my heart
And go walking beneath the enormous sky.
I would like to pray.
And surely of all the stars that perished
Long ago,
One still exists. I think I know
Which one it is—
Which one, at the end of its beam in the sky,
Stands like a white city...
—Rilke, Lament

The stars in the heavens gonna show you the way . . .
—Follow the Drinking Gourd, spiritual

ome years ago I went with my brother to see an Imax film about life in the sea. It was a spectacle in 3D, the screen one hundred feet high. My brother and I sat in the huge theater, with 3D visored helmets over our heads. We must have looked like space travelers, vintage Buck Rogers, ready to scale the night sky.

In the depths above us, clouds of metallic mackerel, drawers and drawers of silverware, sliced through the cobalt water. Thousands of squid spawned, then died, their tissue-like corpses tossing on the ocean floor. Throngs of creatures darted and dove, feasted and rose. The action was larger-than-life, a vision of enormities, galactic entities soaring across the deep.

Here is the part I can never forget: A legion of spiny sea stars, seemingly fashioned out of pastel pipe-cleaners, scrambled to escape a giant sea star. Like animated tumbleweeds, each person-alized by its own ache to survive, they scurried to outrun the colossus bearing down. In the frantic scramble I began to feel a serious dread as if I too were one of the spidery creatures. They were hands dragging themselves along the ocean floor, their appendages gripped and crawled—so many fingerlike limbs trying to amble faster, so much unsuccessful effort. Ironically the whole escapade was impossibly beautiful, the spindly froth of kicks and curls was like a puppeteer's chorus line. The red star was an indiscriminate killer. It mowed and devoured, and kept on mowing.

Why did this vision undo me? Where in my soul had I known such ultimate resignation . . . or such tyranny? Were these entities lodged in my limbic system, the atavistic Titans of eat-or-be-eaten? I constellated some terrible meaning out of that footage. I saw something in those stars.

* * *

A constellation is an event in the mind, a configuration, a grouping of random occurrences, lassoed by the viewer into an image. Light travels from a few bright suns to our eyes, photons settle like dust motes onto our retinas, and we construct an assemblage, bigger and more congruent than the sum of its parts. And if there is no one in the woods to perceive it, it never happened. " To constel-late" is what we do. It is the reason I write, to aggregate disparate elements, to configure a similarity, to essay meaning. It is also the reason you are now reading. It is the course and purpose of our flinting synapses.

The seven brightest stars in the constellation Ursa Major compose the Big Dipper, otherwise known as the Plough, the Chariot, the Drinking Gourd. This first constellation I ever identified as a child is still always the first that I see. Last August, Eamonn, the young boy who lives across the road from me in Ireland, peered up into the night sky and, pointing to that configuration, exclaimed, "Look! The Sauce Pan!"

Because the ancient Arab astronomers were the most thorough in the task of naming the heavens, the stars in my connect-the-dots pot have Arab names. Alkaid is the first star in the panhandle. Where a cook's thumb might go, at the curve in the grip, is actually a binary star, celestial Siamese twins, Mizar and Alcor. Alioth continues the line of the handle to the rim. Megrez, at the rim of the pot down to Phecda at the base . . . Phecda to Merak at the bottom of the pan . . . then Merak up to Dubhe at the lip. Voila! A line from Merak to Dubhe extends to the North Star. Which is how, by following the Drinking Gourd, American slaves were able to plot their way to freedom in the North.

What human could amble out from her home, be it cave or condo, and gape up at the star-strewn night, and not configure the constellations? Who could peer into that fathomless glitter and not hallucinate a form, a face? The sky demands our projections.

Love, too, incites our imaginations. Its promise and mystery hover out of reach like a prize hidden behind a curtain. Beyond that veil we envision a world of enchantment and terror. Celestial seraphs and submarine phantoms enact our primal psychic dramas. The beloved, the object of our desiring, is continually transmuted by our imaginations, one minute a goddess, the next a gorgon. Who is that woman? Indeed who am I? How can one take the trance—transference, transmogrification—out of loving? Can we see the beloved free and clear of all our gobbledeegook? free from the habit of finding her both ruthlessly, and rapturously, divine? How, if sight is ever restored to us, do we know the other?

* * *

Imagine for a moment a tale of such a paradox. You are an adventurer, a sailor, drawn to a shore by a woman's beautiful soprano. You are desperate to find the angel whose melody pulses like a beacon from the harbor. You moor your ship as night falls, and follow her song. At last you come to a tower surrounded by brambles, her candlelit chamber like the moon against the starry night. You search the undergrowth in vain for a doorway at the base of the tower. And then you hear the other voice: "Let me up, you insufferable cunt!" The beautiful singing stops, and in its place is a rasp like rough stones ground into gravel.

"It is time for your dinner, bitch. Let your hair down!"

What monster could make such a fearsome racket?

"Now! or I swear I'll let you starve!"

From your hiding place in the shadows you can see the ladder of tresses cascade, the follicles shimmering like sea foam. You see the crone scramble up like a crab.

What an envious witch, to keep such beauty hidden from view! Poor maiden, you whisper, to be held as a hostage, to be so alone.

For a fortnight you spy on this captive and her keeper. By day the maiden sings, then at night the crone comes to silence her. Oh to touch that delicate skin, her full soft lips, her long fingers. You know you can not live without holding this angel in your arms, without seeing her dear face in the moonlight. How could you doubt her beauty?

* * *

Projections anticipate the external world. Snouts, hairs, tendrils, and thorns all extend through space in order to make contact. They jut and jab, grope and wriggle, for the simple goals of being: to feed or to fight, to know or be known. Projections also exist in the invisible, though no less real world, predicting droughts, bear markets, an early frost. They cast themselves into the future or the past, scheming for ends, both good and bad, and rehearse or review the means. Projections are the limbs of the imagination, the antennas, the horns, the strong legs and opposable thumbs.

* * *

One night you stand at the foot of the tower and call up to her. The witch has not yet come and there is still time. You know how to cause your beloved's hair to spill from the sky: You recite the crone's words. "Rapunzel, Rapunzel, let down your hair!"

It falls like bolts of fabric around you and you begin to hoist yourself up. Your fists make ropes of it. It is like a great net and you, you are its catch. You pull yourself higher, closer to the stars. Oh, it will be heaven when you reach the top, when, at last, you behold each other!

* * *

Look up at the sky, doesn't that cloud look just like a snail? a galloping steed? a smoking gun? Jesus' face was recently captured inside the froth of behemoth cosmic clouds—"star nurseries" they were called by the astronomers who were His unwitting paparazzi. To my mind those clouds looked like coral reefs in some intertidal zone, and the face, well, to me it looked more like Lincoln's. De gustabes. Hallucination is part of our natures; the universe is our Rorschach.

Who can blame us for casting the stars in our personal dramas? It cannot be entirely misguided to believe the elements of the cosmos are interconnected, wound in an enormous contraption: each cog—ourselves included—made up of the same stuff. It stands to reason, given this common denominator, that the arrangements of heavenly bodies reflect something of our own minuscule fates. "I wish I may, I wish I might. . . . "

We try, as Shakespeare said, to find fault—and lost possibility— in a sky full of twinkling stars, aka those behemoth nuclear furnaces. Yet, as Shakespeare went on, the accusation is best turned toward ourselves for the cause of our limitations. The stars are stars; constellations are mere figments of perspective, constructs of a vivid imagination.

Sometime we see a cloud that's dragonish;
A vapour sometime like a bear or lion,
A tower'd citadel, a pendent rock, . . .
> —Anthony and Cleopatra

Projections are our forte, but also our downfall. Our imaginations play tricks on us. How many entities, separate and distinct from ourselves, have been mistaken in nearsighted folly? If we, like Narcissus, cannot see the pond for our reflection, how can we know the depths beyond our skin? How can we hope to distinguish marshland from mirage? mermaid from manatee? Ling cod from Lochness Monster? friend from foe? Projections are meant to inform us about the Eden outside the sheath of our flesh, but more often they describe the interior into which we've been exiled.

History has a way of showing us how misled we have been; how confident we are that this year's fashions will endure, only to find ourselves by next year, an emperor in imaginary finery. Zeitgeist is merely the breath of the time yet, my god, how it feels like *Truth!*

We see, often, too often, what we want to see. Even the bellowing specter of self-made hell must be fussed over like a fetish, as precious and potent as any great work of art. We choose to commit ourselves to it, if only because, like the Big Dipper, it is what we revisit each night, the habit by which we familiarize the dark. The Promethean gift of our imagination is found at the heart of most tragedy, the real weapon discovered at the crime scene. Why would we fashion such horrors?

How did this happen that the very organ of our humanness—as nostril is to dog, as sonar is to bat, as pupil is to owl—would dead-end us with confusion, false information, self-obsession? Would an elephant hang itself with its trunk?

We project—at the very least—to anticipate and taste what we cannot touch, molecule to molecule, and—at the very best—to live out the Golden Rule, heart to heart. We each spend a lifetime struggling to bridge our detachment, to belong, at last—to know the Other.

So what gives? Why do we do such a dismal job of it?

How do we become so dazzled, so blinded?

* * *

It was, by Helen Keller's own description, a life on ice, a bleak wintry world. There was no experience of past, present, or future. She was imprisoned by silence and a never-ebbing dark. Even those who most loved her had lost hope. Then, as she put it, her "brain felt the impact of another mind."

Most of us know the story, how the teacher, the miracle worker, spilled water into one hand, while into the other she spelled "water." The moment rang with its synergy between the two parallel realms of experience, one corporeal, the other cerebral. The marriage of left and right hemispheres resounded. It shone, it glowed, it thawed Helen's landscape and set her free. It brought her into the life of being, in her words, "human."

This was a miracle to be sure. But that's only half the story.

* * *

A woman is impregnated without insemination. A man walks on

water. A loving touch restores mobility to the lame, vigor to the plague-ridden, eyesight to the blind. Bushes, trees, stones, even people spontaneously rupture into flame. The sky lets fall fire, toads, bread soaked with honey. Worldwide, on the same day, statues of a Hindu god drink milk their supplicants leave in bowls. In Spain seventy thousand witness the sun dancing before them. A comet announces the birth of the messiah.

Statues turn to flesh. They weep, they rock, they whisper. Flesh turns to salt, to stone, to ash. Armies are summoned by the Virgin in the clouds. Seas part.

People are abducted by alien creatures and taken onboard spacecraft for medical experimentation. Elvis is spotted in a Midwestern mall. Patients in psychotherapy recover memories of Satanic Ritual Abuse in childhood. Children accuse their teachers of sexual abuse and the school staff is put on trial. Sympathizers are blacklisted. Witches are broiled at the stake.

Hysteria is Faith's stepsister.

Wheat from chaff. Forest for the trees. Baby from the bathwater. How do we know the difference, extract blessing from curse?

* * *

You climb over the window ledge, and peer into her chamber. You can see her silhouetted there, against the far wall. Her hair is like a carpet rolled out before you, a channel of silks stretching to the dark portal of her face. Your arms open to bring her near, to hold her close, to taste her perfection. "It is I . . . your love," you say by way of introduction. The room has an echo. It is colder than you'd expected and there is an unpleasant smell. The scratchy drone of rock begins, "I don't know you," it says. It is deafening, this grinding sound, why is it here among all this softness? "I know my room, my tower, my song, and my keeper . . . but you . . . you are an intruder!" She moves toward you and into the shaft of starlight falling from the window. "I should kill you," the hag grumbles. Her face is grotesque, her flesh scaled like a fish, her hair an enormous tangle of kelp. What choice do you have but to throw yourself out of this tower, away from this horrid sight, and into the brambles?

* * *

Once, all creation was oracular. The skies told stories and issued commandments. Stones, plants, and animals divulged their secrets. In that awesome cosmos miracles were everyday and we were wholly engaged, not yet detached from nature. We belonged to that wise and animate world, and those conversant, if somewhat psychotic voices had not yet exiled us into the secular quiet.

Now we know too much. Fascination recedes. The sky is mute. We are able to know our "selves" as perceivers. Nothing speaks to us because we have come to an understanding that the external world is soulless, that "myth" now means unfounded, fictional, untrue. As Annie Dillard says, "It is difficult to undo our own damage, and to recall to our presence that which we have asked to leave. It is hard to desecrate a grove and change your mind. The very holy mountains are keeping mum."

We can no longer enter into enchantment with life, we enter into a meta-relationship with it—we "interpret" our dreams, reconstruct the narratives of our pasts, hold ourselves at arm's length. In the doldrums between the psyche and world it inhabits, imagination exists like a creature in a zoo exhibit, subject to the scrutiny of the intellect, deemed both quaint and a curiosity. With no access to its natural habitat, the psyche paces without purpose or dignity. Like Rilke's panther in the Paris Zoo, its circumambulations are, "a ritual dance around a center/in which a mighty will stands paralysed." Imagination is trapped, obsessive, unable to fulfill its nature.

Metaphor, of course, survives as a shard from our former preternatural genius, but few experiences still invite that specialism in us. Only love demands the full lexicon of enchantment. We may pathologize this mania from one end of Bedlam to the next, recoil at the way it seduces us, sucks us into its illusory muck. It *is* madness to be sure . . . in love we step into the vital heroism of our dreams. Love is feral and frothy and full of grace, and, by god it is our muse. We see things in it.

Look: We are suddenly no longer living in, say, Los Angeles, circa 2000; we are instead living inside a fairy tale! We are given to another sight. Yes, we have become blind to our solid and steadfast habits, blind to the familiar precincts of our limitations, blind to the outward appearances of our selves! We no longer recognize our faces, nor are we recognized by those who knew us. We step into living and become transparent; we . . . disappear!

* * *

It is very dark, but she finds you. The brambles have cut your arms, legs, and chest, but especially your face, and your eyes. My god, after seeing such fright, all else might as well be gouged away. Your faith in everything—by which you mean your faith in love—has been torn. You are as blind as Oedipus at Colonus, Milton in Paradise, Monet at Giverny.

She is there beside you, and as you cry for lost beauty you feel something other than your own tears. It is her tears, and they plop, one by one, into each of your eyes, washing it clean, restoring your sight.

At first there are just the simple shapes, the movement of light against dark. Her face radiates above you. You strain to see her. It seems her expression is both candid and alien, as familiar and fathomless as the moon.

* * *

Helen's second awakening occurred years later. She was sitting in a library, absorbed in her own imagination. "I have been far away all this time, and I haven't left the room!" she exclaimed to her teacher. She had just been, for all practical purposes—as physicists say of quantum phenomena—in Athens! How was she able to travel beyond the confines of her body, to penetrate—like the mercurial neutrino—the walls of the library and soar across the seas? The spirit, she answered herself, must have its own life.

Only months before she had asked her teacher "Why can we not see God?"

The physical world, her teacher explained, the world of appearances, the world known through the limits of the senses, is a kind of a veil. To demonstrate this, the teacher made Helen stand on one side of a screen, while she stood on the other. "She could not see me and I could not touch her," Helen said, "Yet by little signs I knew she was there, only separated from me by the 'veil' of Japanese paper."

* * *

People will always see things: the ghoul in the pine wood paneling, the genitalia in the river rock. Jesus' face appears one week on a refrigerator door, the next in a photograph of newly hatched galaxies. Mary demurs from a tortilla.

We not only see the things we believe in, we also believe in things we do not see. Black holes are, as far as most of us can comprehend, as fantastic as any sci-fi schtick; so too: subatomic particles, the Unconscious, the super ego. Nevertheless these "entities" shape our world as surely as any vengeful Deity-who-ever-sent-forth-a-scourge-of-plague-upon-the-flat-earth ever did. As if to complicate matters, physicists tell us that things are actually "tendencies," "probabilities." We find ourselves at the mercy of our atavistic metaphors, all the while sensing the existence of things beyond our ability to detect them.

Technology boasts the authority and ability to cause the unseen to appear before us. Yet tomorrow, say, we might watch the film *2001* or the explosion of The Challenger, and wonder which is the most virtual. Which happened really: men walked on the moon? Buddha dispelled an army of demons by touching the earth?

We are in the dark, grasping at holographic straws. Can we explain how the parts of the atom are pulled together? What exactly is that cosmic muscularity that forces mass into attraction with mass? What exactly causes the northern lights? And while we're at it, what is light? How do we know another human being? Indeed, why are we curious, fascinated, determined to know Her despite our formidable handicaps?

* * *

One November night a few years ago I was in a jet from Ireland to New York. I peered out the teeny window to find the Northern lights undulating in Day-Glo green below me. The drapery was hung from the bowl of the Big Dipper, and both seemed to be suspended below the horizon, an apparition in what I assumed was the sea. I had lost the horizon, was entirely disoriented in the night sky, like those pilots who aim their planes into a fatal nosedive. It was a spectacular vision, but one that filled me with dread. The curtains of the aurora unfurled and furled like sheets of cream poured from the lip of a saucepan, but did this portend disaster? where did the sky begin and the sea end?

I thought about my beloved and the undersea things of our relationship. Such dread I've anticipated at the bottom of our love: a shark's fury, an eel's grin, the defeat of a legion of sea stars. I could sink and drown at such depths.

It is one thing, one quite horrible thing, to be lost amid the hall of mirrors of your own skewed vision, to suspect that your feeling of disorientation is not merely a trick of the mind. You know you have the Mortal Dread within you, and you know how it can cause you to envision the worst: ghastly chimera over the sea and in the skies. It can contaminate the very thing you hold dear, make love itself seem monstrous, unworthy of your best efforts to see beyond and through its most despairing mirage. It can, in effect, make you believe in witches, and in lovers forever held hostage by their own limitations.

It is quite another thing to accept your sight for what it is, to know the ways in which you will hallucinate, either out of love or out of fear. Was it necessary to always "understand," was it necessary to always find a "meaning"?

I beheld The Drinking Gourd, the beacon that guided refugees from human bondage. And there, at its rim, was the enigmatic veil, the aurora borealis, rippling in its own mysterious breezes. What did I make of that irridescence? Love or fear; fear or love? What I saw from the porthole of that plane was an invitation to enter into a world I cannot control or understand, to follow love's perplexing song and let it undo me, if need be.

"No pessimist ever discovered the secret of the stars," Helen Keller reminded me. " . . . Or opened the doorway for the human spirit." Either sunk in our privacies, or soaring in our efforts to touch, the blind lead the blind.

what endures

Parrots, tortoises and redwoods
Live a longer life than men do,
Men a longer life than dogs do,
Dogs a longer life than love does.
—Edna St. Vincent Millay, *Pretty Love I Must Outlive You*

There are days I can almost believe
the marriage will last, will seam itself
and last, and the stars will sing of this
to starfish, in the language that they share
because they share a shape.
—Albert Goldbarth, *Natural History*

Not just for an hour,
not just for a day . . .
—Irving Berlin, *Always*

L ove, the kind Ms. Millay refers to, that odd hybrid of lust and devotion, the thing some call romantic, some marital: This is the thing about which longevity is in question. Can, does this love last? We are not asking does all love last. Not asking does love of friends endure, love of work, nature, parents, siblings, God, surely not love of children, no. We are deep in the woods of questioning the love that stokes our popular songs, our movies, the thing that worms about in the understory of our most secret thoughts, our fantasies. The demanding, however transient, feeling that goads us to reach for four hundred thread count linens, the SuperSmile

Toothpaste, the "Obsession" perfume. The directive that makes us speak our lines out loud. The passion that motivates the most brutal murders, and that draws us, myth after myth, to the underworld.

Why have we come to this place in history when we dismiss this love as simply romantic, vulgar, pathological? yet are at the same time eagerly manipulated by the saws of song lyrics, or films whose scores swell to coax the lump to our throats? Why, in the deepest darkest recesses of our hearts do we believe that in being in love we are in a state of Grace? that love is our Quest?

It seems my ventures into romance were as fleeting as breakfasts: Hungers once riveted the pathos to the foreground, demanded absolute attention, but once the plates were cleared and time passed, can I possibly recall the exact flavor? Am I really that fickle? What endures? I like to think of myself as a person who comes to love with devotion, whose tenacity precedes all laziness, irritability, or capriciousness. I hate to think my character is as flawed as the zeitgeist's. But these days displeasures are easily disposed of, what becomes obsolete can be flushed down the drain or trucked off to the recycling center. We can always upgrade, get the new model. The newer, the better.

We're advised at every turn we should feel good. We struggle to "have" and honor our feelings, as if feelings constituted a substantial treasure, more precious, more dear, than even the Other. Sacrifice is translated into self-betrayal, yet conflict is simply intolerable. Feeling good about ourselves has become our rudder, and every journey we embark upon must be navigated according to comfort and fulfillment, elsewise it is judged to be a misadventure, even self-destructive. But who among those whose marriages last would report a lifetime of comfort?

I was weaned on countless episodes of *Divorce Court*, and however much I saw myself as a crusader for marriage, I was, in fact, the poster girl for serial monogamy. Three years, five years, two years, seven . . . my former enchantments strung behind me like past lives it would take a medium to dredge.

But now the jig is up. Here I am, newly fifty, and I require sudden mutation. I have stumbled into a state of undeserved grace, love has knocked me on my kiester and—MAYDAY MAYDAY—I need some kind of personality transplant, some crash course on commitment, some wise words. Who can instruct me? Who in this world knows about being, and staying, in love?

* * *

Vivian Gornick in *The End Of The Novel Of Love* announces that love, as a force of radical transformation, is dead. Postmoderns are now free to pursue any and all experience, able to chase our fulfillment, and Love, divested of its threat to bourgeoisie coupling, is no longer the agent that can "put us at the center of our own experience."

Love no longer has the power to "create a rich, deep, textured prose out of the ordinary reports of daily life." We can, I suppose, do it on our own.

So why not, as Lillian Hellman said, change lobsters and dance?

* * *

Once upon a time the kingdom was soft and bright. The membrane of the castle was as transparent as ectoplasm, and shone in the sun like a bell of blown glass. At night the castle radiated, and the activities of the young princess were apparent for anyone to view. Light spilled from castle hill and into the town below. Those were the good old days. That was before the Dark Ages, before the briars grew riotous, and the brambles brandished their thorns to all passersby, before the walls of the castle became opaque and dingy, and the beacon that had been Castle Hill was as lost in the night as an imploded star. It wasn't so much that our princess was comatose, it was simply that she was perpetually asleep: whether walking or cooking, eating or spinning, she was in a dream.

But fear not, believers, 'cause soon comes the valiant suitor, the one who would stir our princess from her routine oblivion. Of course it will take more than a machete, a bugle call, or even a perfect kiss to penetrate our numbed heroine. Upon waking in the arms of the beloved, she will have to learn all the lessons she missed in her decades of sleeping. How to kiss back, for starters. Next, how to stay awake.

* * *

When I was growing up there was a novelty toy, a plastic eight ball that could foretell the future. You'd ask a question, shake the thing and peer into its small window of inky fluid. In a moment or two a message would float up to the window's surface: *Yes, definitely* or *It will take some time* or *Don't bank on it.* Now it seems that I retrieve the past in such a manner. More recently it takes longer for memories— the names upon names of school chums, teachers, acquaintances, favorite authors—to drift up to the surface. They take their own sweet time, these corpses in the bog, unmoored from the will of recall. Given a little time they may float up into the mind's eye, or onto the lips, . . . or not.

Some bits are lost forever. Gone are the dates of the signing of the Magna Carta, the end of the Civil War. But there are others, held closer to the heart, that once, I swore, were indelible: birth dates, death dates, parents' anniversary. They too evaporated like the once unforgettable contours of a lover's smile. Worse, many of these memorials can't even be jogged by reexperience. Would I recognize, blindfolded, the flavors of a 1995 Brunello? The texture of an ex-lover's skin? What shock to reread a poem and feel that I've been dropped off in a foreign neighborhood. The only thing familiar about it is the astonishment, once again, at being lost, that I must relearn the territory from scratch.

I say all this because, while we may grudgingly accept the body's frailty, it is hard knocks to reckon with the soul's infidelities. What, if anything, stays with us? Does anything memorialize itself? What was that last thought?

* * *

Our stalwart suitor has just kissed our sleeping princess. Oh, it is a lovely thing to awaken someone with a kiss! Her eyes open with surprise, gratitude, and surrender. But then, in a moment she has drifted off, her lips slacken, lids drop like an exhalation. Oh, her pillows are exquisitely soft, the afternoon light narcotic. The chamber's familiarity is soporific. With every little snore the brambles scale the bedroom window valence.

The suitor is bereft and angry. How deep and tenacious is this trance? This princess is a princess after all, and life has become so comfortable, so routine in its satisfactions, why should she struggle to be otherwise?

* * *

What I've known about marriage from the union of my father and mother is that it can be a stage for soliloquies, a lectern for the recitations of innumerable betrayals. I did not witness intimacy in their union—my formative, larval cosmos—only one kiss in a kitchen, and once my mother hiding from me behind my father in his bed. Few laughs, no conversational thrall, no friendship. No winks, pinches, no come-hither looks.

I heard the din of jaw grinding, saw the beleaguered litter of martyrdom hoist upon their shoulders. They were unhappy for as long as I can remember. I learned to anticipate their resignation, and so it came to live inside my own body. I know it's not supposed to be that way. I've heard stories.

I see the vows of marriage, the architecture of commitment, but I'm stumped by what must it be like to live inside it. "To love, honor, and obey." What does that mean? Whenever I've imagined speaking those vows, I felt stymied by the notion of honor, and shuddered at the idea of obedience. Obedience represented enslavement, indeed seemed at the very crux of female oppression within the patriarchal institution of marriage.

Now as I ponder a marriage between two women—supposedly cootie-free of the patriarchy—I wonder what could possibly encourage two people, particularly my beloved and me, two characters with egos to beat the band, to stay together. Can L-O-V-E do that? Can love be bigger than the ego?

How to love, honor, and obey without the ego being always at the wheel, and always, as the ego is, asleep in dreams of itself. The ego is intoxicated with feelings, it wants, it cries, it hordes betrayal, it seeks to punish, it craves power. But aren't we supposed to obey our feelings? Isn't that, in part, what we are working so hard to recover in all our modern practices of psychotherapy? Can love be stronger, *other*, than feelings? What is love then, if not a feeling? Why—if it is other than a feeling and if it does not speak for the feeling Self—is love a big damn deal?

And what's so necessary about this coveted Self, since its lauded emotions can be upstaged by love, since its destiny is merely moth-like, to be charred by the illumination it craves?

Love, contrary to Ms. Gornick's proclamation, is indeed a Quest, a journey in which we immolate the myth of ourselves.

* * *

Since the blast of Creation, everything in the universe is scattershot and farther flung, breaking down to dust, shrugging off heat, cooling, slowing. Observation shows us that all things atrophy, the bearings grind, the knees creek, the gate is rusted off its hinges, and even memory ain't what it used to be. Why should love be any different? It, too, must surely run its course, behave like any other thing we've studied behind the lenses of our micro/tele/spectroscopes. (Mustn't it?)

Of course, under the press of time, while we watch our chin hairs grizzle, the lure of the nonscientific, of the airy-fairy metaphysical, turns downright torrid. Even the word *everlasting* sounds as scrumptious as mother's milk. We desire that *something* should last; indeed that something should outlast us. And if it cannot be that our names persist on the lips of those who survive us, that our accomplishments simply fade into the dazzling, ever-upstaging background, at least this then: the legacy of a headstone or a small bronze plaque, the surname etched for all eternity. Me, it always pronounces, me, I loved once. (But might there be more?)

The bones and teeth are the last to disintegrate. Dig up the cat two years later and you will find the ochre skull with its pointy canines, the elegant tibias and fibias, the vertebrae still as snugly strung as pop beads. The rest will be dirt, proof that God is just, that nothing will be wasted, that new life will be granted a feast.

This much, beyond the shadow of a doubt, is lasting. (But couldn't there be something else?)

The bodily remains of the holy are vessels of the Holy Spirit . . . so contended Thomas Aquinas, himself a saint. Among treasured reliquary we find the shoulder bone of St. John the Baptist, the teeth and jaw of St. Anthony, Buddha's toenail, a hair of Mohammed. These are proof: The Spirit, as evidenced, lives. We need proof, surely, as we must have foci for worship, surely as we crave a lifeline in the sea. (What endures?)

* * *

OK, you know how the story goes: our hero has to follow our heroine down into the deep dark world of her oblivion. If they survive their doubts, the temptation to look behind them, they make it out of Satan's muck into the bright light of a spring day. Don't ask me how it's done, I'm still trying to learn.

I do know theirs wasn't a onetime journey, they had to do it many times, and it didn't get any easier. As some Sufi once said, in typical sufitude, "If you are seeking a spiritual practice . . . fall in love!"

What I do know is that there are four forces that govern us. Forget what the physicists say—they will inevitably change their minds, make discoveries, cut a swath for the new zeitgeist. Forget the Weak Force and the Strong Force; forget Z particles and the rest. There are four: Sex, Death, Vanity, and Love.

Sex is the glue. The titillation that keeps the elements engaged. The stuff of orbits, magnets, luscious apples plopping in the dust. Bodies are continually in thrall with one another. Take the sensual embraces of the garden snail, roiling slimily bosom to bosom. During their amorous grind one of these bisexuals will pitch an arrow of spermshot, a dart into the bilge of its twin. It can't be helped, they're powerless over the spell of attraction.

But then later, when they're served up on a plate with butter and garlic, their flesh is in service of something slower and colder— that we may remember the earth's musk, the cycle that, in time, manufactures soil out of even the farmer. Another of nature's commandments: No one leaves alive.

We think of death as a singular occurrence, a moment when vital signs are leveled to a horizontal streak on a screen. It's the curtain falling, the end of a story, the Klieg lights turned off with a shudder. Of course after THE END is superimposed over the curtain, after the finale has reached its coda and the audience is headed for home, there's someone winding up the reel, sweeping under the seats, dragging out the garbage. Death has occurred but that's not the end of it. After we're dead we may be gone, but our bodies, or I should say *those* bodies—no longer ours, no longer beholden to the entities we once were—*those* bodies have begun a new undertaking. They are now committed to entropy. Instantly the surface of the cornea clouds. Once distinguished by a unique mission in the body, each brain cell, lung cell, toenail cell, now proceeds to drift toward communal decomposition. Identity— "toe," "lung," and "brain"—is a thing of the past.

So you, too, friend. Soon enough, with the help of so many dermatodes, springtails, maggots, and microbes, you too, will be composted. But don't take it personally. Death is a much more gradual process really than the itty-bitty snuffing of our individual lives. It's our Sun's slow dimming, the ebbing of Heat. All the bright babies coalescing, falling back into the body of the dark mother.

A chill may, in fact, be in the air, so you draw that shawl tightly up around your neck, and contemplate your insignificance. Much of your life has been in service to Almighty Vanity, but now all that emotive tyranny amounts to squat. That diva in the mirror had been a strict dominatrix, she made you wed yourself to her every impulse, made you cowtow, even made you applaud. She ate up all the scenery. You wanted everything to mean something, and you wanted it to go on forever. There is no shame in that; it was part of your nature, you couldn't resist it.

Take some comfort here, assume our lives, complete with all their dramas, are sewn like beads into the garment of something colossal and continuous. A curtain, perhaps, like the aurora borealis. Identity, powerful as she was, is folly, a bright but lesser god. There are bigger fish to fry.

Here's where Love comes in.

Here is your spark, your Grail, your conflagration. Don't tarry, friend, this is what you were born to: Start your pyre and throw yourself upon it.

* * *

Long after Sleeping Beauty and her beloved died, the legend of their love lived on. Some said the light from Castle Hill became a constellation in the night sky, and that the light from those stars would shine long after the earth's cities dimmed and froze. Why, reader, do you now snort at this as if it were a simpleton's fairy tale? Why can't love outlast us, make a palpable constellation somewhere in this knowable universe? Why should our hearts disbelieve what our souls intuit, insist upon?

Look up. You can almost trace the constellation of the Kiss. There, can't you see it? The suitor bent to waken the princess? And see . . . her shining eyes the two brightest stars in the heavens?

* * *

I've never heard the death rattle. To have been spared (or denied) its rasp at middle-age is another strange development of post-modern life. What might have been the propulsion for a word sputters, a weave unraveled into random, incoherent, threads. Just air escaping the lungs for the last time. In the interest of blind optimism, and the desperate hope that it's not all been for naught, let's affirm the seam of marriage.

Yeats wrote a poem about withering into the one root, one truth, he called it. I am reminded of a couple, Roger Williams, founder of Rhode Island, and his beloved, buried together near an apple tree. When they were later to be dug up for reburial, it was discovered that their corpses had been wholly consumed and replaced by the apple tree's roots, their flesh forms supplanted by their root doubles. In the pitch of their reopened grave, their root-pale proxies glowed like binary stars.

In the end what endures, what isn't converted by the alchemy of dirt, is made up of the bits of ourselves we've placed outside our bodies: the stuff we've stored in museums, libraries, songs, vows—and, I believe, in the ethereal plasma of love. Such enduring love requires more than most us humans can handle: patience, gratitude, honor, and obedience, which in turn demand flexibility and the struggle to stay awake. It is, like death, nothing short of transubstantiation, the conversion of clods to spirit, prose to song, doldrums to glory, and it requires impossible, daily belief. Nevertheless we'll go to bat, and believe that sea stars will be serenaded by their heavenly doubles. And then too, just to be safe, we'll consult our meager oracles; *Don't bank on it* they will whisper, or *Yes, definitely,* or that sure bet, *It will take some time.*

Love will outlast doubt, death, and decomposition; because, my dearest, my gallant one, we make it so.

the prospect of wholesomeness

Some thoughts on Self, Nonself, resistance and respect

> I married me a wife
> She's the plague of my life . . .
> —Traditional Folk Song

> But Love has pitched his mansion in
> The place of excrement.
> —Yeats, *Crazy Jane Talks With The Bishop*

> Surely I have eaten many a tart that fell to the floor before it felt my plate, and more
> than a hundred bowls of soup whose temperature was tested, consciously or not, by a fat
> thumb. I have even pushed dead flies to one side of an omelet or ragout, and eaten to the
> last bite undaunted. I have not really minded, inside of me, because what I ate was good,
> and I do not think that good food can come from a bad kitchen.
> —M.F.K. Fisher, *Serve It Forth*

*I*t shone in the glass more than any I'd ever seen, and small beads of cream, almost butter, bobbed at the top. What kind of milk *was* this, I asked. "Fresh," my hosts instructed, fresh from their cow. "It's better than any of that store-bought stuff . . . better for you, too." My playmate, in whose home I was invited for lunch, threw me a superior look. His mother smiled and passed me the plate with its heap of egg salad sandwiches. These, too, were entirely exotic, their yellow filling Crayola bright.

My parents' reaction to my story of lunch at Wayne's house took me by surprise. Didn't I know you could get sick from fresh milk? or from fresh eggs? "Germs," they kept saying, followed shortly by that word "unpasteurized." "You must never eat anything from Wayne's house again!" End of topic. Message received: Good things, pretty things, things tasty and, especially, fresh, could do me in.

Jump cut to another tale involving yellow: I was seven, plopped slack-jawed in front of the tube, ogling a movie that gave me nightmares, one that piqued this budding mistrust of things that seemed benign, but weren't.

Old Yeller featured a stalwart golden retriever, his tongue draped heroically from the side of his mouth like an aviator's scarf, who rescues his towheaded master from an attack by a wolf. The wolf is monstrous, the dark aspect to the blonde dog's saintliness, villainous and brutally wild. Worse, he's rabid, which codifies his ferocity, distills his evil. The boy is saved, but our hero, bitten and bloodied in the fight, is now infected with the virus and must be put down. The sad, unalterable transformation from goodness to evil, from loving to out-of-control, was a fate that seemed, at my age of seven, to contradict what I believed about nature. I had assumed the world, with minor exceptions, was safe. Evil things—like the wart-nubbed witches who foraged for children—revealed their natures in spectacular ugliness. But I was learning that appearances are deceptive.

A quick twist of the dial and there sits Louis Pasteur aka Paul Muni in a starched lab coat, hunched over his microscope, peering into a mob of anarchic bacterium. The year is 1880 and the yellow flags of quarantine are nailed to Parisian doorways. While the disease-ridden of Monmartre wail and foam outside his laboratory window, the dedicated doctor toils by day and by night, to discover . . . not only a cure for infectious diseases, but to defend the world against its new foe, the germ. He discovers staphylococcus, streptococcus, and pneumococcus, and persuades the medical establishment that invisible agents can create large-scale

catastrophes, that itty-bitty organisms, too small to be seen by even the
microscopic eye, are the agents of cholera, anthrax, and rabies.

Unbridled and imminent evil exists everywhere, both these
movies declared, and it can fester undetected in the most benign
places . . . on the tongue of a dog, say, or within a sip of milk.

But it doesn't stop there. Evil penetrates not only realms of the
minuscule, it goes to the very soul of things. Today the little photo
of Pasteur in my dictionary resembles the one of Sigmund Freud,
another Fin-de-Siecle genius, another prober of the subversive
realm of the unseen. These two Victorian Pandoras, bearded and
baggy eyed, have given me reason to mistrust. Nothing is what it
seems, and few things are guaranteed safe. The floor is dirty, the
mind, unclean. Who and what can you trust if not the ground
under your feet or the voice inside your head?

* * *

Are ideas and images, like germs, dangerous? Can they infect our
souls? cause corruption?

The acquisition of knowledge requires that previous lessons be
learned, some cognitive, some ethical, some developmental. Most
cultures have rites of passage for coming of age, initiation rituals
for "mysterious" or "occult" wisdom.

Our mythologies are rife with stories of knowledge that is
forbidden, that backfires into cataclysm when fallen into the
wrong hands. These tales seem to say we are too steeped in pride
and self-deception to ever be trusted. We now know the risks of

splitting the atom, splicing the gene, Solomon's koan of hacking the child in two, and yet . . . we're always sure we'll be the ones to know what's best. We're inevitably blind-sided by the feeling in our bones that, dad gum it, we're *right*.

Then, paradise would have been ours, if only we hadn't . . . lifted that lid, stolen that flame, spied a God in the lamplight, taken that bite. . . .

* * *

Let's imagine a different scientific scene, a different attitude in the course of scientific inquiry:

Our hero, Barbara, is hunched over a microscope, looking at chromosomes inside a cell of corn starch. She lifts her head, takes off her glasses, and faces the window. "My god," she whispers, to no one in particular, "they are jumping!"

It is the spring of 1948, a stormy day in Cold Spring Harbor, Long Island. She is middle-aged, skinny, short hair, plain as a potato, though she'd probably prefer to liken herself to a cob of corn. She is staring, not really looking at anything, absorbed in a mental replay of what she's just witnessed down there in that jewel-like cell. In her mind, she is the same size as that cell, able to stretch her arms around the diaphanous wall of its cytoplasm, place her cheek against the pillow of it, and listen. She is so quiet she is barely breathing.

She's fond of telling her students, "Listen, always listen, and sooner or later, the plant will speak to you."

What this woman, Barbara McClintock, has just seen with her very own eyes are changes occurring inside the cell's chromosome: Genes are moving, the structure of genetic information is changing, the mechanism by which evolution happens just happened. This moment and trillions more just like it are the triggers for mutation among the species, occasions for new life to originate, Nature keeping her options open.

But this event, miraculous though it may be, is not what Barbara is ultimately listening for. What she is listening for, and what she will spend the next forty years of her life listening for, are the reasons why. These glistening, chubby spheres, who jiggle around her like fertility goddesses, and who's gelatinous company she cherishes above all other's, are telling her of their ability to recognize their imperfections and to correct them, they are telling her they are self-regulating, they are showing her they are wise.

Of course, what sane person would believe such a conceit?

. . . Cells, wise?

It hardly matters. For Barbara to have become this no-frills genius, she's had to grow up unruffled, unfettered, but still curious. She's got immunity to disbelief, indifference, scorn even. The cells change, she knows, as a response to stress, what she calls "challenge." She's an intractable old coot, old maid, cob of corn, and that, dear skeptic, no matter what you think of those teeny, brilliant cells, is that.

* * *

A good thing: antibiotics . . . like, say, streptomycin the cure for tuberculosis. A bad thing: antibiotics . . . like, say, streptomycin, which thirty years after "curing" tuberculosis has generated a new, resistant strain. It's a Frankenstein story, a comedy of karmic errors that would make poor obsessive-compulsive Louis Pasteur roll in the seethe of his microbial grave. His germ theory, which revolutionized surgery and obstetrics with its holy commandment of sterilization, couldn't anticipate the super germs mutating around the evolutionary corner. It is not enough, apparently, to zap the lurking agents of infection. Immunity is much more subtle.

Who among us, who grew up in the antiseptic households of the Mid-Twentieth Century, would have predicted the recent medical uses of leeches? Or maggots? Who would have foreseen that in the twenty-first century intestinal parasites, like Helminth worms, would be used to treat inflammatory bowel disease, one of the new klatch of autoimmune disorders? Parasites require of their hosts a healthy symbiosis. It's in their self-interests to perform useful tasks around their home. They bolster the body's immune response.

We do not seek an environment that is scoured of diseases, but rather one which does not overpower our own resistances to them. Once the flora has been too pinched, the fauna too clipped, once the balance has been tipped, the immune system, like the environment at large, is more vulnerable to infection. Nature seeks homeostasis amongst the widest possible diversity. Look at our graphs depicting the planet over geological time, how she survives catastrophe after catastrophe: the spires of hot ages, the scarps of ice ages, life forms either morph or succumb, but life again and again, ad infinitum, amen.

Immunity could be viewed as a martial art, a dance of respect and resistance, a struggle for balance. We tend to see it as a militia's bastion, an all-out barrage, Armageddon.

* * *

I recently saw a photograph from the 1999 World Press Photo Contest: a woman in Bangladesh lying on a bed with her infant child. I could not recognize, until I read the caption, that this grotesque on the bed is, in fact, a woman. She is disfigured beyond recognition by an attack in which a neighbor had thrown acid on her.

At first I could not even bring myself to look at it for more than a second at a time. I had to take it in small bits, force myself to keep glancing at it, then look away.

She is lying on her side, her arm braced over the child who is staring blankly upward. The camera is at eye level with the woman—if she had eyes, that is. What she has, and what is so ghastly to see, since our looking always begins by locating the eyes, are two bulbs of flesh that protrude from the collage of tissue that once was her face. I searched for similes for those knobs: figs? sea slugs? It is pointless. They once were eyes and now they are . . . untranslatable.

It is difficult to know for sure what the woman is feeling, since all means of facial expression have been excoriated from her. Any speculation, though probable, is pure projection. She is struck down, scarred beyond my ability to stomach it.

The baby too seems afflicted, though less visibly, benumbed by the colossal agony into which she's been born and about which she can not possibly, nor perhaps ever will, comprehend. She seems the incarnation of bewilderment, of resignation. Her eyes and mouth, the black areas of the photograph, are voids.

Speechlessness is, in sum, what this photograph amounts to: the silence of its subjects, and of any viewer's reflex to them. Then there's the vacuum-like question of why . . . or better: How can any human being do such a thing? What makes it possible? The caption reads, "eight to ten acid attacks on women are reported every month in Bangladesh." Later, "She was eight months pregnant at the time. . . . "There are, of course, all the extenuating influences, institutionalized misogyny, just for starters; but cruelty—and this is certainly just one snapshot of it—is common among our kind, no matter the time or place. Any human being can do such things, apparently.

* * *

"Eat me," "bite me," we say as the ultimate insult, a kind of na-na-na-na insouciance, meant to disarm another's rage on the most primitive level. You can not hurt me! I'm impervious to you!

It's not brutality alone that scares us, bullies kicking sand in the face of the skinny guy, big fish gobbling the smaller one, on and on, down the line. Oh the shark bites, with his teeth dear, but so does the plague-ridden flea, no bigger than a poppy seed. Then there's the contra tenor mosquito, always ready to spread the wealth of its microbial bounty around. Dog bites are bad, not to mention the lip-lock of tick. And the problem is seldom so much the wound as the chemistry involved in the gnash.

Kisses, too, pack their sizable perils. Viruses of all stripes emigrate across the oceans of our saliva, and before you know it, you and your beloved are both coughing up phlegm, down with the flu.

Same as with combat, you take your chances with love. Contact, necessary as it is, also can bring corruption. Someone walks into your life, and it turns out she's unwittingly smuggled contagion from the old country—not just her viral history, but a whole load of psychic vermin. First there's the unpacking of the tales, fantasies, interests, and values. Then the more virulent stuff lurking at the bottom of her duffle: the ghosts of pugilists, assassins, child-emperors, professional critics. In no time you are both looking a bit like mother Bates, midstab. Everyone knows one good turn deserves another, an eye for an eye, a jugular for a spurting jugular, and soon the whole love nest is fouled, booby-trapped, frigid as a prison watch tower. What kind of arsenal do we require to survive our intimacies?

Our most famous pathologies are our defenses gone berserk, the alarm switch jammed in the ON position. Phobics know how threat whispers from each sidewalk crack and unwashed doorknob, how only the most dedicated can perfect a system to prevail. Counterphobics know to eliminate the source of the problem altogether, and if, like Ted Bundy, they make a grand splash of it, how much more the victor! It's just us and them, my friend. And you, too, are beginning to look a bit strange.

Each cell inside us has a marker that identifies it as "our own," something like a security badge or a key card that allows it to peaceably coexist within the cellular community of our bodies. Whatever appears as an intruder, as a bit strange, sets off our immune response, and the trespasser is set upon by antibodies. Sometimes, and for some reason—especially now—our immune systems can wrongly identify cells.

Before twenty years ago did we know about, or did there exist, such horrors as AIDS, lupus, Epstein-Barr, chronic fatigue? Did we talk about our immune systems or autoimmune disease? Not to mention the gauntlet of potential allergens that menace with infinite variety, from mite turds to peanuts, horsehair to red dye number two? As never before, the world has a contract out on us. We gotta watch it. We're now required to pack our dust masks, air filters, rubber gloves, water purifiers, inhalers, sanitary wipes, burglar alarms, car alarms, zappers, pepper spray, bulletproof vests, telephone listening devices, voice scramblers, motion detectors, grenades, revolvers, rifles, automatic weapons. . . .

* * *

It is the spring of 1999. I am standing outside a refugee camp on the border of Kosovo and Macedonia. It is what you might imagine: people standing at the gate with their worldly possessions stuffed into black plastic garbage bags, staring through the hogwire, waiting to be let in. They are, by appearances, scruffy and sleep-deprived. Inside the enclosure, behind the fence, are tents, people cooking their dinners over open fires, men smoking together . . .

staring out through the hogwire at those who are staring in, a few children playing in the distance, the shit smell of latrines.

Only a few yards away is the border crossing, a stretch of road between the two officiating gateways of exile and entry. This warm afternoon only a handful have crossed into Macedonia, as opposed to the four thousand just days ago. Then their walk across this road was a gauntlet of inquisitions from immigration authorities, media piranhas, exhausted relief workers, and war crimes investigators. This quiet bodes ill for those who remain behind in the mountains of Kosovo, who are either in hiding or captive or worse.

Later, my friend and I walk down the road away from the border, the way we came, toward Skopje. The evening air is soft and filled with the buzzing of insects. We see a tortoise, big as a helmet, strolling the tarmac. There are several flattened lizards, with verdigris bellies. Butterflies are everywhere. And all along the brush as we approach, we hear the scurrying of small animals making their getaway.

This part of the Balkans is unspoiled. There is no development, no smog. There are no power lines, no road signs, no fences. It is difficult to reconcile this calm and unencumbered landscape with the atrocities just a few miles north. I am speaking not only about the infamous acts of systematic genocide on the part of our recent enemy, the Serbs, but also of NATO's miscalculated, as well as intentioned, offenses—the defilement of roads and farms, the poisoning of soil and water, the litter of cluster bombs left in fields identical to these, so serene with their daisies and birdsong.

Soldiers step out of the bushes a few yards ahead of us, their

Kalishnikovs draped over their arms. I am afraid but I slip my focus into the familiar comforts of nature, peering harder to this side and that, trying to identify a flower, a bush, a tree. My companion is alert, she finds her defense: Her strengths are in attention to relevant detail, in being fully awake. I am alert to all else, to the distant sound of the cuckoo, the chirrup of a finch. I am riveted to this realm of beauty, to steady myself, to hide my fear from these soldiers—and from myself. I even hum a tune.

The men are young and you can almost smell the hormonal prestige their guns and uniforms have given them. They approach and ask for our papers. They seem to enjoy detaining us, making us unsure. They like their power. They are sucking it like they once sucked their thumbs, like my friend and I are now sucking—in a figurative, but still on our knees kind of way—their testosterone inspired authority.

We are let go, of course, after a little military spooking. However much these Macedonians are sympathetic to the Serbs, however much they may resent the intrusion of up to 250 thousand refugees onto their land, their official business is to support NATO's military effort. Our bombers growl northward, unseen at altitudes high above this valley. The cuckoo continues to make its call. Time to be going.

It is difficult to imagine how we could make this paradise into such a hell, or for that matter, how the Serbs or the ethnic Albanians could have stoked their incendiary abuses for literal centuries. "Why" is the mantra that calls from every cranny of the landscape, unrelenting as the cuckoo.

It is easy to remember the whiff of sadism I got from the young Macedonian soldiers, as well as my tendency to deny all danger, thus, too, the responsibility of its consequence. I know how to look the other way and hum a tune. It is harder to admit that I have conjured the face of my own enemy from the face of my beloved, my mother, my father, my neighbor, a perfect stranger.

* * *

It could be argued that most human meanness originates from information improperly acquired, a cognitive aberration. Something is missing in the developmental equation: like a sense of self, like a sense of the other, like that thing we call the Golden Rule. Otherwise how could we hallucinate the Other as our Nemesis?

It would be nearly impossible, I'm sure, to shield a child from the corrupting influences that slither even among the most innocent-looking apple boughs. But if I had a child I'd want, I think, to protect her from certain kinds of knowledge. I'd want her to have grit before venturing too far out into the world. She'd have to have some wisdom under her belt before I'd set her loose into the glandular wilds of popular culture. She'd have to be comfortable enough inside her own skin to grapple with the sexual miasma of most entertainment, confident enough in her imagination to meet up with the likes of Freddy Kruger, intrepid as Clarise Starling in her encounter with Hannibal Lector.

How can we give our children—or ourselves for that matter—security, immunity, grit? Surely the solution can't be to cringe inside an airtight bubble or to arm ourselves to the teeth.

Delivered fresh from the duct, mother's milk is about the most nutritious food on the planet, sterile, and, except in a few instances, filtered of toxins. And, importantly, it comes with its own stock-pile of medications: antibodies that assist in the child's immunity to whatever perils its geographic region will throw its way. This transportation of immune boosters between mother and child via breast milk is called "passive immunity." Lymphocytes and Gamma interferon strengthen the cellular fortress, lymphocytes and macrophages aggressively attack microbes in the baby's teensy gut. In the laboratory, breast milk will cause even cancer cells to die. Breast milk has all the right stuff, but its greatest nutrient is undoubtedly psychic. New life does not thrive by milk alone.

Albeit rigged to dispense milk, the wire monkey mother is less desirable to the baby monkey—hapless specimen—than the wire mum done-up in terrycloth. The wide-eyed infant will cling fero-ciously to the expressionless mannequin, squeezing out whatever molecules of proxy mothering its love-starved simian brain can, because . . . the big numb surrogate is, AT LEAST, cuddly. Cuddling is essential to survival, equal, if not more sought after than milk.

If our baby ape was reared by a living, breathing mom, it'd glean through imitation, interaction, exploration, and play about all things apish, all the while secure that this affectional body will offer comfort, authority, protection. The craving for cuddles never leaves our mammalian heart—being close gave us the sustenance milk alone couldn't. Beyond our survival, closeness gives us the freedom and security to become ourselves. Love, intimate contact, is the environment in which we grow. Physical affection is crucial for the formation of our sense of security, the development of our intellectual aptitudes, our dispositions, our abilities to assign appropriate values to things—to distinguish, for example, a mountain from a mole hill, to recognize an "us" from a "them," or most immediately, a "thou" from a "you."

* * *

Call it passive immunity, or simply the milk of human kindness, but a story came to me recently by way of my beloved, the one with whom contact is most profound, and with whom conflict is most potent—the one who knows my vulnerabilities and resistances, the one who's seen my fangs and tasted my blood. It's a story that I take with me into my everyday world, whenever I need to consider the dynamics of reciprocity:

A village was once terrorized by a snake. Every day and every night the snake slithered through the village and bit whomever displeased him. Some children had died from the snake's venom; some villagers had lost their limbs. No one knew what to do. Finally they sent for a holy man.

The holy man came to the village and saw the suffering the snake had caused.

"Take me to this snake. I must speak with him!" said the wise man.

The villagers were skeptical for, as far as they knew, no one had ever spoken with a snake. Nevertheless, because they were desperate they took the holy man to a cave in the mountains where they believed the snake lived.

A few days passed, and then the holy man came back down into the village.

"You are safe now," he said, "go about your business in peace. The snake will no longer harm you."

"What did you do?" the villagers demanded.

"I have shared my wisdom with the snake and he is now enlightened. You have nothing more to fear from him."

Sure enough, weeks passed and the snake attacked no one. Months passed happily and the wise man, travelling nearby, paid another visit to the village. He saw the people about their business, children playing in the streets, flower pots in the windows, signs of economic upswing. Though happy for the people, he had come to visit his disciple and could find him nowhere. Finally he climbed back up to the cave. There he found his student in a horrible state. The snake had been beaten and kicked and spat upon. His skin was shredded, his tail flattened, his eyes gouged. "My god," exclaimed the wise man, "What has happened to you?"

"You taught me enlightenment," said the snake, "Now I am changed. I can never bring harm to any living thing. And no matter how people beat me and kick me and spit upon me, no matter how vengeful their cursing, I remember what you told me and will not strike at them."

The wise man shook his head.

"I never told you not to hiss!"

Here's what I know about paradise: Sometimes you have to be in exile to recognize it, to distinguish what's holy from what's "for granted." I continually encounter this when I'm in Ireland. When I'm there I feel closer to the kind of experience Barbara had when viewing those dancing cells. She too was a foreigner, a blow in, Gulliver among her glittering centrospheres. And what she saw there was herself, after a fashion. For example:

Kate and her son, Eamonn, now ten, are flirting. Kate is hanging
out the wash on the line, and Eamonn stands beside her like a
nurse next to a surgeon, slapping each clothespin into her palm
like a scalpel. Eamonn picks up another clothespin and mimes a
tweak to Kate's nipple. She grabs it out of his hand. "I'll pin this on
your waggle, I will!" she play-scolds, chasing him, to his squeals of
delight. There is no mistrust here, no dark secret of incest, no anxiety of inappropriate behavior, none of the discomfort I see in my
culture, where fear nearly always triumphs over trust. This is not
the *Jerry Springer* show. Each person in this vignette has a self, a
boundary, a trust that is reinforced by the playful suggestion of
transgression. Eamonn, Kate is saying, you will soon be a man, but
you will always be safe to be my child. I know and respect myself
and you, and therefore . . . love.

* * *

*What would Barbara make of those who, even with the best of intentions,
toy with her miraculous genomes? Who, with no respect for mystery,
would turn a deaf ear to them? "The parts add up," she repeats, "The cells
are wise for a reason." They self-regulate according to "controls," as she
calls them, some unseen Oz over the rainbow, above the cornfields.*

*She takes off her glasses and, with a soft clack, places them on the
Formica table. It is now the summer of Love, 1969, fifteen years after her
discovery of transposition in the chromosome, of "jumping genes," and fifteen years before she will receive the Nobel Prize for their discovery. Her
eyes automatically trace the dried cobs of corn on the ledge of her laboratory window. Some are uniform and yellow; others are variegated, pebbled*

like ancient mosaic. Her vision has shifted away from her happy Brobdingnag—this telescoped realm where translucent sylphs meet with her, belly to belly, and initiate her into their mysteries—to the actual scene outside in the harbor.

It's the August moon glissading across the bay, illuminating the water, the trees, the other buildings. On the opposite shore, the darkened Eugenics Record Office crouches under the pines. Closed since she began working at Cold Spring Harbor, it remains as a relic of scientific inquiry gone way, way, awry.

Tonight a manned rocket has set down on that big bright lunar ball, in a place called the "Sea of Tranquillity," and soon a man will plant his Mylar boots on its dusty surface. They will look to our intrepid scientist like two steaming foil bags of Jiffy Pop. (She enjoys seeing corn in everything.) "One giant leap for mankind," the Michelin man in Jiffy Pop boots will say, accompanied by a fair amount of space-culled static. Who would have thought we could come so far?

To what realm would Barbara's research propel her? She has traced the evolution of modern corn from a simple grass, she has pioneered ethnobiology, she has identified "telomeres" the ends of the genetic ribbon that fray, then repair themselves (until old age makes them cry "uncle").

How far a distance—after her very-own telomeres have given out and ceased to rejuvenate, after her cells wither up and break down into carbons, after she is dust fit for the likes of foil booties—would the work with genomes go? Her colleagues will produce bigger, better strains of, among other things, corn. Then, who knows? better fruit flies, mice, and . . . blonde haired Über babies? Of course, there will be research into anti-aging, anticancer, all the good stuff, with the best of intentions. Lives will be saved. Generations will prosper.

But can we be wiser than the cells themselves? Or whatever Oz it is that wrangles their controls?

Pitting wonder against piety, our Socratic plain-Jane recites, "I don't know" often. The root of the word obedience means "to listen," and this she does with daily devotion. "Things are much more marvelous than the scientific method allows us to conceive," she says. So our ascetic stays close to her microscope, her keyhole to awe.

No matter if we spoil the seed record, undermine the immune system, and even—with the best of intentions—reopen the Eugenics Records Office, her friends, the cells, will still be at it, rising to the challenge, reshuffling their chromosomes according to unseen controls, keeping the big options open, behaving in ways we can't anticipate.

She looks away from the window, puts back on her glasses and tunnels back to paradise.

She will receive many awards in the following years without enthusiasm. The publicity will spoil the solitude, interrupt the silence it takes for her to hear the cells speak.

Isn't this the trick of God? To see the woof and the weave? To respect the self and all that is the nonself? To relinquish hatred but still stay defended? To remember how to hiss and stay in love? To be flexible enough to leap, yet maintain homeostastis? To keep the whole in mind among the many? Isn't this creating a boundary, a self, a world? Isn't this loving? wholesomeness?

apples

> *Like the sweet apple which reddens upon the topmost bough,*
> *Atop on the topmost twig—which the pluckers forgot, somehow—*
> *Forgot it not, nay, but got it not, for none could get it 'til now.*
> —Sappho, translated by Dante Gabriel Rossetti

> *I'll give my love an apple without a core*
> *I'll give my love a dwelling without a door*
> *I'll give my love a palace wherein she might be*
> *That she might unlock it without a key. . . .*
> —Traditional folk song

Remember the first, there in the dappled light: the bauble, hung like an ornament on the bough. Doesn't it dazzle, all green with its tarnished navel? You draw your hand up through the leaves, grab the fruit without trepidation, with surety, firmness. It is the object of your desire, the aim of your id, treasure for the grasping.

Mine is a Pippin, plucked from a grizzled branch in the orchard. Its skin is tough and my teeth slide around on its surface before I can latch into it. The skin finally cracks, and my teeth shovel the flesh. The flavors are both sour and tannin. My mouth is one part juice, the other dry cotton. I enter its world.

How does it happen that apples imply worlds? That apples bode an inward passage to places not unlike the body? To eat of the apple is to break through the membrane of another dimension. Its skin resists penetration, then yields. It announces its surrender with a snap and plash, like a dive into water.

Jump then, take a bite. Consume this body, swallow its juices. Its pale flesh is a host on your tongue; and profane, secular mysteries—not God—are decoded by your spit. "This," offers the everyday world, "is *my* body: human, animal, mineral, elemental. Know me, enter the appellation of your hungers, know yourself."

See the woman reaching for the fruit there in the Garden? See her soon-to-be-husband standing beside her, before the advent of appetite, naked, chaste, inert. This is the moment before Pandora's figments are loosed upon the world. It is the moment before they say, "I do," before the perfection of love is corrupted by its tasting; the moment before they are sent away like Odysseus to engage the world's terrors, long before they find their way home.

This bliss, this pre-Fall love is as drab as a mealy winesap, its depth must be earned by flavor, by spice and suffering. All the stories tell us that. Whatever the consequence of wanting and of eating it, the apple is always meant to tantalize, always Aphrodite's enigmatic offering, a female's koan. Its arrival in a story portends that Love's strict lessons will soon be instructed. The apple belongs to Love's Teacher. Look at Her desk, littered with the gifts.

Our heroine's eyes light up as she savors that first bite, as the juice drips down from chin to collarbone. "Here," she purrs, prodding him with her treasure, "taste." In the words of *TV Guide*, trouble (necessary, inevitable) ensues.

Lovers beware!

* * *

For all its dangling engorgement, its yielding rupture, its spilling juices, the apple is interchangeable with genitalia. And there, they'd have us believe, at the bull's-eye, at the flowering and the fruit of our flesh, is the germ of our rift with God. That fruit, the story goes, is a revelation, first of nakedness, then of shame, and from there an avalanche of sexual misconduct. The Latin word for both "apple" and "bad,"*Malum* is evil in its rudiment, Eve's fruit. One taste changes everything.

Another interpretation is that, at the very least, that morsel must have been some kind of antidote to aphasia. For when the proto-couple take the bite, they wake from dreaming. They now are set upon by a fever to name each posy and pooch, each emotion and molecule, and soon the garden looks a lot more meta than physical. They carve their runes into stone, scribble their sonnets onto paper, digitalize their hypertexts onto the World Wide Web. They are primary subjects in a realm of now-distinct objects, and with each new word-tchotchke, the garden is further objectified. In no time they themselves are Other, self-conscious objects in a psychic Diaspora.

In either version, whether the knowledge is sexual or cognitive, the apple's flavors swing wide the gate, . . . and see? there you stand with juice on your lips, a weird terrain unfolding before you. The truth, it's said, can set you free. But freedom also exacts a price, innocence can't be recaptured, and exile, regardless the revelation, is the lonesome consequence. What a toll, after all, to grow up.

The apple then becomes an emblem of paradox, both sweet and sour. On one hand it is embodiment itself, the delightful world of crunch and infusion, a realm of floorboards, solid tabletops and known quantities; on the other, it hovers like a hologram beyond our grasp; if tasted, we wake to a whole new landscape, . . . and where did the apple go? Fascination is forever goading us to reach, to clasp, to hold, to taste . . . but by definition it resists satiety—just as mystery continually evades discovery.

* * *

Christopher Columbus was said to have had his the-world-is-round moment when he compared the sails he saw on the western horizon to the silver back of a moth he watched ambling over the cusp of a sphere. I like to imagine that globe as an apple in his hand. Some variety like a Cortland or a Rome. I like to imagine he took a bite as he dreamed of his course due west of Gibraltar, before his encounter with the New World.

Two centuries later, in the mere blinking of an eye, his inquiries reveal a world utterly changed. It's doubtful Columbus would even have recognized it.

The year is 1666, and a traffic of ships is mapping arcs across the globe, navigating crossings to and from the Americas, steering by the stars. Their

holds are loaded with slaves, zealots, immigrants; with explorers and colo-
nizers; with exotic plunder and stowaway vermin. Look at the markets
teaming with chocolate and tobacco; churches encrusted with gold! Look
at these European tables now set for a king . . . tomatoes, squash, sugar,
and corn.

There is, however, a dark consequence to this age of exploration.
Another round of plague is razing Europe. It has spread from ships to
cities, and from cities to towns. In London over seventy-five thousand
have perished. The streets are stymied with rioting and rubble, with
stench and fire.

But miles outside of London, on a tranquil lane, in a quiet garden
under an evening sky, another man is in contemplation of an apple. The
scene sounds bucolic, except that this young man has no desire to be here.
London's university is closed for the three years of this national disaster
and, since he's young and penniless, he's got no choice but to return here,
to live with his mother in his mother's house.

There is no air in Mrs. Newton's house, and no wind in Mrs. Newton's
garden, but within the stillness the universe is taking on a new shape.
Isaac is tracing this new form within the recesses of her apple trees.

An apple is falling, and as it impacts the earth, dust shoots up like a
bowl around it, then settles. To our young genius, it's a conundrum.

Another apple succumbs, and another. . . . Succumbs to what, Isaac
wonders.

Suddenly his mind is reordered and refreshed. His thoughts are
infused with the possibility of a different cosmos: The planet's body has
an irresistible command on the bodies of other things—man, apple,
dust. Even objects further up are obedient to its authority, the topmost

fruit of his mother's orchard, the swallows in their evening sweep of the sky. The moon, as it happens, is also pulled toward this same dusty ground. The heavenly spheres are caught in attraction for one another— orbits, ellipses, the sun, the moon: The whole cosmos obeys the apple's same MO.

Nothing is falling really. . . .

* * *

It looks more like Illinois than France, but France it is. Rose and I are driving over a rolling plain of wheat fields, under a stratum of troublesome clouds. We are following the rifts in that gray blanket, hoping to find a peephole to the sky, meandering the motorways northwest of Paris for a view to the total solar eclipse. We see an island of sun off the starboard side, and steer a course ever more northward.

Some minutes later we drop anchor at a sunny intersection between country lane and dirt road. We have charted our position to be in the line of totality, the area at which the moon's shadow will cut a swath across Europe and the Middle East, and at which those in its umbra will witness the sun's blot for several minutes. We park and appraise our surroundings. To our *droit* is a razored wheat field, perpendicular stalks-on-parade. To our *gauche*, a corn-field, aka green Alhambra, aka, impromptu toilet. Right ahead is a small forest (good since we wanted to hear the birds' hush at totality) and behind us a few miles to the south, the ribbon of motorway with its tributaries leading to small towns in the distance.

The sky is widening and we call upon our inner pagans to improvise chants and keep the skies clear.

During the hours that we count down the eclipse, other cars pull off the road, each a respectable distance from ours. Many people set up telescopes, picnic lunches, and folding chairs.

A farmer in his tractor turns onto the dirt road, and approaches our car. We hold out our bottle of wine to him as he passes, flashing his tusky smile. He lets us know with a wave of his hand that he'll forgo our offer and that we're welcome in his field. Clouds of dust rise from the wheels of his trailer as he calls out something to us about the rat race in the city. He's carting manure, seemingly unconcerned about the last astrophysical pageant to occur in this millennium. He has—if not seen it all before—then seen it previewed on CNN . . . besides, today's a workday.

I am thinking about his double from the last millennium, a toothy Gaul hauling manure with his oxen. It is May 5th, 840, and, with no CNN, no worldwide heads-up, there are no folks staring skyward anticipating an eclipse. The day is like any other spring day. The bees are abuzz, the birds are calling from the forest which, except for a few cultivated clearings of wheat, stretches as far as the eye can see. What did that farmer think—after a lifetime of everyday, every year rhythms—when the sun disappeared from the sky?

* * *

When I met Rose I hadn't a clue that I'd be waking into a state of exile. I dreamed the same safe dream of a child, under the spell of my own design, a narcotic of life-as-I've-always-wished-it-would-be. Call it innocence or stupor, a princess could spend her whole life asleep. And the cure? Wake up, grasp the hand of your beloved and walk away from the castle of your childhood.

But it's never as simple as a fairy tale. Not easy to walk away, not easy to stay awake, not easy to keep the beloved's hand in one's own. And of course, love too is bewitchment, a fantasia that knowledge can dispel at one tasting.

It is bitter knowledge, indeed, to discover that the beloved is a figment, dreamed out of our earliest, most infantile wish.

So who is that cantankerous, frustrating woman who continually holds out her hand? Can I know her as she desires to be known, stripped of my hallucinations, naked as the day? The hinterlands beyond the gate, it turns out, are chockablock with conflict, difficult to negotiate, hardly what I hoped. And once I have this knowledge, and suffer the ancient dismay, will I still—can I still—walk with her, in Grace? Do the revelations of intimacy banish one from the garden of desire?

Wanting implies loss. If we crave the cookie, it's a sure bet we envision a world in limited supply. This is the nursery-old terror: to be denied. Thus we are gun-shy and trigger-happy, poised for the next "Dear John." One whiff of trouble and—Poof!—our hands wrest a wiggle of smoke in the air.

What have we fallen into, but our own aloneness?

Such falling is hard—but how else could anything so priceless not also be expensive? How could anything so heartfelt not also put us at risk? Why wouldn't the latest rebuke not mirror our very first?

* * *

One can only imagine what life had been like when Isaac was younger. His mother's house, his mother's garden, his mother's misery. What kind of despair would make a mother give up her child? He must have heard witches pacing the ceiling, must have seen the walls fracture, and watched objects fly at tantrum velocity. She left Isaac in the care of her parents when he was a toddler. When they died he was returned to her, only to be farmed out to another foster home. Then back to her again; then off to another. . . . One can only speculate how—regardless of her own hardships—the tidal power of those vacillating commitments formed him: his renowned insecurity, his famous temper, his nervous breakdowns at thirty-five, then at fifty. Both precipitated by the possibilities of new love.

One can only imagine how on this quiet evening—as he listens to the thud of fruit on the ground, as he grapples with their plummet from every angle possible—his thoughts might also be influenced by the power of his own rage and ancient longing.

What is gravity, what is this behemoth force that keeps all things in its tether? Isn't it as contentious, as quixotic as a mother's love? Isn't that pull as central to our notions of "up-ness," "down-ness," "here-ness," and "there-ness."

The sun, the earth, the moon, the human heart. Which force exacts the fiercest tug?

* * *

As the moon begins to occulate the sun, we climb onto the roof of our rental car to stand, back pressed to back, our eyes scouring the dome. All the things they tell you happen: It gets dimmer, the drone of insects and birds hushes, the stars reemerge and the ribbon of highway primps like gemstone gaudery. The light mutates into hues you thought impossible in the nondreaming world—a ghostly spectrum fanning from violet to silver.

I look down at the stubble of wheat to my left—it is purple, flecked with gold. The former colonnade of corn to my right is now like a polarized photograph, in which the shadows of leaves are more livid than the leaves themselves. The air is still, expectant, cold; and her back is warm against mine.

My experience of the eclipse begins to gel into something I can only describe as "antithesis." I had expected this moment to exact a sharp thrill, to be distilled into some preternatural laser. In fact, it is its opposite, . . . it is soporific. I feel that, like the bees, like the birds, I am being called to bed. I find my thoughts unraveling, my perceptions slackening. I am under the spell of some cosmic Mesmer, and I struggle, if vainly, to hold reason together. This time-lapse evening, which falls so swiftly and without the home base of horizon, which spills sensations of dreamlife into waking, has the power to rend me as dazed as a dozing skylark. I try to imagine what this experience might be like for my serf at the advent of the first millennium, and I recognize how this twilight's undertow has the power to invite panic in midday. Were I some snaggletoothed farmer working his soil at the moment of totality, I would think I was dying. . . .Or that God was dying, or had given up, or had fallen into a behemoth slumber, and would never wake.

As it is, even with my knowledge of planetary movement, my CNN preview and Internet prep, I suspect something utterly subversive. I can't shake the dread, primitive, existential. "What happens," my circadian body demands, my medulla oblongata shrieks, "if it doesn't reappear?"

In Greek the word eclipse means *abandonment.*

What would it be like, I wonder, if the duration of this eclipse were more than seven minutes? Like, say, seven hours? seven days? seven weeks? How would we endure the waiting?

The sun or the moon, a God, spring, a groundhog, rainy weather, . . . and Love. How do we keep our faith?

Think of the Peruvian earthworks, their devotion aimed skyward, saying plainly, "We haven't forgotten," and "Welcome back!"

Stone circles, say, or almanacs, Spirituals, myths, legends, songs, vows . . . and marriage.

These seven minutes are beautiful, cold, counterintuitive. I feel her back against mine. I am blessed to share the cosmic scissure with her; to know the day returns even after such catastrophe. We are routinely visited by love, so we have no choice but to believe in the existence of the invisible, in things we cannot see, nor touch. We have known abandonment, felt terror, survived the semidarkness.

This moment is the best way I can think of to describe our marriage.

* * *

Exile defines you. You feel as bruised and as dispatched as an apple fallen from a tree. You hope each nick won't show too much; pray each bruise won't rot you to the core.

Life instructs that all matter of things are taken away—a mommy's love, or God's; a garden, spring, Haley's Comet or a groundhog—they'll either return some day, or not. . . .

But in the interim, Penelope, while you wait for the hyacinths to pop their heads, nail the calendar to the wall, set the photo by the bedside, touch the locket at your throat. The Beloved will come back to you, remember? It won't be long.

* * *

Birds sing in a different language, navigate according to different stars. The hemispheres are at headstands, day is night and night is day. The more we eat our apple, the more it disappears!

So say good-bye to Newton's Eden. Good-bye to the stage where blood n' guts divas wail Wagnerian librettos, good-bye to solid landmarks, and full-bodied thrusts. Let your anchor levitate from the harbor of your psyche, take another bite, deconstruct the fruit.

We chew it down into smaller bits, and at each descending rung of scale our landscape transfigures. So long to the bantam realm of our cytospheres, our worker bee cells, bustling in their watery hives! Adieu to the molecular and the small-fry. We are leaving life in all its corpuscular splendor, so say fare thee well to birth and death; behold a new shore.

Here is a galaxy of hyperkinetic motes, jots, dots, and bitty iotas, all seized with infinite and insensible energy. Particles zing in and out of our vision, propelled by alien, centrifugal laws. This is the real world of cold-blooded force and collision, so get used to it, forget compassion as it was ever described to you; dry your eyes, take a bite, look again.

After chewing it further, on yet closer inspection, those wee specks of matter aren't even there. The new frontier of the sub-atomic is all dynamism, a netherworld of verbs without nouns. But see the trails of vapor those sly verbs leave behind? The footprints of the ghosts as they steal through the snow? Good-bye to sturdy frames of reference even, to metaphors and long-ago floorboards, toodle-do.

Now you know the downward narrative, the paradox of the ever-reducible world, the infinite declensions of "To Be." What truer underpinnings lie beneath this luscious dawn-to-dust? What lingers at the threshold of this next millennium? What visions, what flavors greet us there, just outside the gate?

* * *

Here are some apples for the picking:

Magritte's is midair, obscuring a businessman's face, insisting that mystery still hovers behind the persona of the everyday. This is pure Modernist allegory, an invitation to the enigma of our-selves. Matisse's, by contrast, are shallow and golden delicious, too naked in the morning light, gay as breakfast brioche. Again by con-trast, Cezanne's fruit, like his beloved mountains, are heavy and dense as lead, weighted by temporal dimensions. Piccasso's, too, exist in a different physics, refracting their tumescence, the very monument of rut.

Proust dried and stowed his in a drawer, to be later utilized for a whiff of inspiration. Thoreau's were touted as virile, iconoclasts best enjoyed in the fresh air. Sappho used hers as bait to lure Aphrodite back to earth. Lorca's slumbered in the bowl and dreamed dreams. . . .

* * *

Malum Pumila Paradisiaca, sweet fruit of my desiring, object of my curiosity, fruit of knowledge, of evil, of exile, truest food; most tantalizing mystery, apple of my eye.

When I see her "I love you" on the page my heart leaps up. The words and letters look edible. And like food, they both soothe and quicken me. I read them aloud. The sounds vibrate in my mouth and throat. They fill my body. I read them to myself, and their phantom kinesthesia does the same. The sentence is round and whole and bright and good, cheerful and pleasing (never tiring) as a bauble on a sunlit bough. Oh, care for me, oh, comfort me; feed me with your sweetmeat, keep the doctor away.

It is a holy triad, these words: Primary subject: *moi.* Most cherished, vital verb: *love.* Object of affection: *thou.*

A gestalt, a fullness, a closed system, radiant triumvirate.

Physicists tell us we can further penetrate this apple; and bite through the membrane of time. The apple's "there-ness" (complete with "wormholes") is a space inside space. It's "Is-ness," a time without time. What we end up with is a multidimensional knot of strings, which are really more like vibrations. But vibrations of what thing or what event? Are they flung from the cloak of a Ghost, cast from some surfaceless sea, plucked from cosmic frets? Rilke asked, "Upon what instrument are we two spanned/ And what musician holds us in his hand?/ Oh, sweetest song."

I believe there is something like a current running below this dimension. I say "below" out of habit, the way one might speak of the directions of up and down, utterly defined by the custom of shoes planted on floor, of our earthcentrism, as one thinks of apples falling—rather than flying—toward the earth. But I mean to suggest something else altogether, to direct you toward a coexistant realm, the dregs and flotsam of which we behold as our universe.

There are times when I can almost feel the rush and muscle of this stream, though it has neither a bank nor a source nor a destination. It is not an event and has no duration, not a dot, not a line, not a sheet, not a block. It is, I suspect, something of this thing called "God," and love is just one drop of it.

Do I know this for certain? Is it a fact? Can I feel it, touch it, smell it, taste it?

If love is the intangible, yet consummate verb—as we know in our hearts it is—then who is the object? And who is the subject?

What is the mysterious event called matter? Or its intangible animator: the spirit? What is this beating wet organ, the gory pump inside us? or its metaphysical spouse, also called "heart," more like a wave than a particle? Why are we subject to the physics of our hunger? What are we made of anyhow?

Perhaps we are like the dreams out of which apples sleep, or the paintings that purport their voluble density, all rut, frivolity, enigma, fragrance.

We are figments of our own imagining, if such a paradox can be possible.

And so what can it mean as you stand before me, without a stitch, your birthday suit more real than anything I've ever known? What is this terrible gift you bring, all shiny and bright, ready to be tasted?

other mouths

"You must sit down," says Love, "and taste my meat."
So I did sit and eat.
—George Herbert, *Love*

Sweet as candy in a candy shop
Is just your sweet sweet lollypop
You gotta give me some, please give me some
I love all day suckers, you gotta give me some
—William Spencer by way of Bessie Smith, *You've Got To Give Me Some*

I, who am food, eat the eater of food!
—*The Upanishads*

*O*f course the first orifice was not the mouth, not the bellows spout, the pump sucking the sky, working the breast. Not the trumpeter of "mine." At the beginning, despite all the brouhaha about the Word, we spoke through a mouth at the belly. The navel was the causeway of all need, the course of life's infusion, the first source of the unconditional. Now that knot's a fossil, a cowry's cast, an imprint of life lived in a forgotten sea.

Once upon a time in that brine, in the paradise which had no names for "me" distinct from "She," symbiosis lived at the root of your being. Being and relation were the same. Now a centrifugal scar marks the rebuke of exile, the harsh start of your struggle to survive on your own.

The bittersweet memory of being larger than your self lurks at the belly button, like the sensations of a phantom limb. What you once knew at this nub was substance, mainstay, telepathy; as well as the terror of being jettisoned like a spaceman from the capsule. But here was also your license, your embarkation into privacy, the bittersweet excitement of drawing into the distinction of you. The navel is the stem of the fruit: the place of becoming—that is, both of breaking apart and of breaking free.

Then your nerves assumed control from your mother's body. The umbilical vein atrophied to a ligament around the liver. The stem at the center of your body shriveled and—now, here you are—an apple fallen from the tree.

The fruit yearns for the tree, and because of this, it produces seeds. Thus an apple will spend its life growing into not just the lauded filler of pies, nor the bauble of our eye, but the chrysalis for the nascent tree. Come hell or high water it will be reunited with the Life Giver, the Greater Thing, wholly whole once more: branching, rooting, in Grace, a contained container. We all will. Each body exists in enthusiastic perpetuity, in which seed begets a seed, either in fast forward or in reverse. One form transmogrifies into another; clay into claymation; or dust—after a Nijinsky flourish—dust.

And what is that vehicle of transubstantiation—be it the tongue for the melting host, the canal for the crowning head, the grave's maw for the corpse—but some kind of vamp on a threshold? Through navel, ear, cunt, or anus, we are a conduit for all that is not us, a siphon for the gifts that go and come, unbidden. Likewise, we move, dissolved and digested, through the guts and gears of the Other, through the eye of the beholder, or the leviathan bowel of Oblivion.

In thinking about other mouths, or channels, or ingress and egress, we come to the narrative moment, the end or beginning of the story. Out or In? Isn't the earth the portal for Jesus, Orpheus, Persephone, a cub, a crocus, a groundhog? Each is risen up out of the dirt, or birthed out. Or is it rather that, like Jonah, Jesus, Aladdin, the family guinea pig, we all are perpetually brought to the reckoning within? To be swallowed by fire or decay? Of course it is, finally, that like Jesus, Persephone, Orpheus, Adam, Dante, the Golem, the door swings, seasonally, both ways. The mouths we have, and those into which we are subsumed, are more mighty than the entities we imagine ourselves to be. Up, down, inside, or out—as the Hindus say: It is all food.

* * *

The first meal we cooked for Kate and Bill was probably our best, by which I mean, the one *they* liked.

We had lived in Ireland across the road from them for over a year. We had all spent many a night in the pub in conversation, trying mightily to render a few intelligible phrases from the babel of our accents, becoming, over time, familiar with each other's temperaments, humors, and values. We talked in oblique, and then not-so-oblique, ways about sex and politics, discussed local and familial issues, astronomy (Bill's secret passion), being in love (they have been since they were teenagers), even, finally, our friendship. But we had not yet ventured into the territory of sharing a meal together. The subject of food often came up: about which local fish were good, about a few of the ways to cook a potato, about the merits of Guinness and of Coke, about sweets, biscuits, cakes, and crisps, about how we took our tea. Kate brokered us fresh eggs from a woman down the boreen, and Bill offered to catch us a salmon come summer. We discussed food preferences ("I like *plain* food." Bill emphasized, " . . . very plain.") but it was already clear that, despite the fact that we watched many of the same television programs, grew up in roughly the same generation, and spoke, roughly, the same language, our nouns and adjectives would provide us limited understanding of each other's tastes. Our hungers were as odd to the other as our accents.

For months Rose and I fantasized about having Kate and Bill and their four kids over for supper, yet we always found a rationalization for not. The middle room of our small cottage contained, among other things, the fireplace, the computer, the sofa, the sink, the fridge, and the stove—and though the locals have been cooking and eating and entertaining and sleeping in just such rooms for centuries—it felt too small to us.

One afternoon Kate called from town to tell us her mother was sick in the hospital. Rose got off the phone and said "Kate's not going to be able to get home in time to fix the kids their supper. Let's make a meal and take it over." So we spent the afternoon cooking a lamb stew. We used the computer table to bone the meat and chop all the vegetables. We rendered the fat, and browned the meat and softened the onions. We added some stock, carrots, and potatoes, and let the whole thing simmer for a few hours, then threw in some peas as a last-minute touch. We skimmed off a few tablespoons of fat for health considerations, but left a goodly portion, knowing full well our recipe would be damned in the States. We took a fourth for our own dinner, and lugged the rest across the road in our big stainless pot.

This was the perfect gesture. Not so intimate and imposing, mind you, as having to bring new friends into your home; but still intimate and inclusive enough to demonstrate goodwill and great affection. This stew said we cared for them, we wanted them to be fed, sated, warmed, happy. We touched them where they lived, but let them experience that touch in private.

The next day as we pulled onto the road on our way to town, their youngest, Eamonn, popped out his front door. "The soup was *luscious*," he crooned, half to give credit-where-credit-was-due, and half to flirt. His mouth curled and spread into a wide grin (his gratitude accentuated by his parenthetical dimples). Rose and I looked at this gaped-toothed, ten-year-old emissary, then at each other, then swooned. What a score!

For weeks we heard praises from the neighbors, who clearly enjoyed the food we cooked them.

* * *

In the primeval organisms the first brain was the digestive system.

Not too hard to figure: matter is swallowed, assimilated, secreted. Ascend the evolutionary ladder and absorption gets a bit more complex, a bit more—literally—cerebral; the senses feast, matter is chewed and considered, we're nourished, and then, God willing, catharsis happens. But therein lies the foundation for aesthetics and sublimation and generations of hungers that, though ravenous, might be as culturally constructed as a prepubescent fad.

Likewise both nervous system and enteric system find their twin-like origins in the genesis of the embryo, when a clump of tissue called the Neural Crest split, one part migrating north toward the cranium, the other drifting south to the abdominal lowlands. Only later in development are both brain and gut connected via the vagus nerve, that super highway linking, among other things, anxiety and heartburn. Brain and bowel are marvels of packaging, twenty-one feet of intestine are all folded tidily behind our insular paunches, while inside the skull, the cerebral cortex is crimped and corrugated to accommodate one hundred thousand kilometers of nerve cells. Both systems concoct a pharmacological larder of psychotropic juices: natural opiates, such as enkephalin; neurotransmitters such as serotonin, dopamine, norepinephrine, nitric oxide; and benzodiazepines—the family of psychoactive chemicals found in Valium and Xanax. It is clear that mouths of different sorts are continually chewing the fat, digesting material, disseminating the essentials.

In either case, whether in consideration of Homer or hamburger, we are meat making careful consideration of meat. Yet, how can it be that simple viscera knows the exquisite moment?

That grist, bone, and marrow can calculate the distance to the moon? This ticker tape of a thought has its address inside the blood sausage charlotte of your brain. That grey pudding can somehow replay Brahms' symphonies within its soft interior. Viscera is the portal through which the mysterious entities of heart, mind, and soul express themselves and palpate the world. Matter, miraculously, celebrates itself.

Given such consideration, is any orifice simply an orifice? Isn't each more like an altar, a laboratory, a theater, a tribunal?

The eye, obviously, is not simply an eye, but the eye of the beholder, the organ of the soul that discerns, selects, forages for beauty, feeds itself in the delights of seeing. Through its mouth we take in the face of the beloved and that vision is being transformed, disseminated, altered by our fascination. We are beginning, in a sense, to eat her with our eyes, to digest her, and at the same time to record her, to archive her. To transubstantiate her from the world of flesh to the realm of fetish.

There is more to our orifi than meets the eye, more than what occurs at the threshold of the pupil, the mouth, the nostril, the ear canal. Indeed, one of our most articulate mouths, the skin, has no opening.

After birth, once the umbilical mouth was closed, after the new mouth yowled and proclaimed itself king, the skin, too, woke up and began to taste. In the new dry dimension, the skin translated "the Other" from the old canon of amniosis to the new lexicon of touch. The first arena of postnatal relationship was never only oral, our sole volume of love's vicissitudes. Flesh became love's other conduit, the heart's sounder, its singer, its favorite site. It fed upon the things of the world. Turned inside out, this sheath contains the guts of the nonself; it is the medium through which the world is most substantially known to us. It is our primary palpus, the heart's open palm, the mouth at the center of our affectional lives.

And with which mouth do we taste another's joy or suffering? Upon which retina do psychic photons settle? Which neuron probes that which lives in another time or place? In what region of our bodies do we experience communion?

* * *

We converted the milking barn into an addition. We'd laid the floor, painted the walls, arranged for Bill's cousin to build us a fitted kitchen. We purchased a newfangled fridge, a stove, and a heavy porcelain basin. We bought a long table, the top made of old oak flooring and put it in the spot where the barn used to snuggle up next to the house, where the pig's room used to be. We assembled eight chairs and eight table settings. So we asked our neighbors over.

We deduced they liked lamb, and therefore stuck to the empirical, "If it ain't broke, don't fix it," menu plan. Bill had stressed the word "plain" so we decided on chops, broiled, just salt and pepper. Spuds were an obvious addition, so we researched the Irish version of mashed potato: a milkier, silkier, rendition called "champ." Sliced carrots, sautéed with a little butter and sugar, rounded out each plate, now a fragrant triumvirate: glossy vegetable, smooth carbohydrate and, the *piece de la resistance,* the chops, prettily pink, cooked to perfection.

Judging by the scowls of our guests the lamb was blatantly uncooked. It seemed to them, I imagined, lurid, pagan, obscenely reluctant to relinquish its animal vigor. The carrots too, having held their shape and texture, were underassimilated. "We like our food cooked well," Kate offered with a wink. Bill made a gracious and gallant try to appreciate the red wine. He took a few sips, blushed a little, and pronounced it "not bad," then never revisited his glass.

I caught the glances shooting around the table. Our guests' mouths were pursed slightly. The barely hidden smirks were tolerant and conspiratory. They had reached telepathic consensus that we, the Yanks, though having meant well, hardly knew our arses from a hole in the wall. This meal confirmed our status as exotic, if somewhat clownish, strangers. I glanced at five plates of uneaten food. Only Eamonn busily gobbled his share, then seconds, then lifted his face to display his dimples. He giggled his pleasure, not just with the food, but with the knowledge that his appetites distinguish him as unique. The rest of us giggled with him, relieved to let our discomforts pass.

So how does one consider the Other, please, when the Other's experience is, as it always is, strange? *That* is clearly not *This,* and no matter how *This* always tries to upstage *That, That* continues to reappear, ever strange. *That* will always evade our knowing.

That is troublesome, its presence chafes the curbstones of *This,* we can hear it pace in the night, and everything contained herein grows restless with all that lurks herewithout. In Italo Calvino's wonderful story *Mitosis*, the protagonist, the primeval amoeba, struggles to transcend its own narcissistic confines. From the hearth of its nucleus to the outer precincts of its cytoplasm, it can perceive nothing but itself, and that knowledge is eventually what vexes it with claustrophobia, what stirs it with lust, goads it toward something other than itself, and ultimately causes it to split itself into two, to become the Other it so desires. This hunger is, Calvino extrapolates, the cause for birth, love, and self-destruction, the hinge upon which Eros and Thanatos swing.

Of course the lives of our egos are similarly confining. And thus hungers can generate tensions between who we know ourselves to be and who we might become, can rend the self to pieces. To see, to smell, to taste, to hear, (to fall in love) . . . all dangerous possibilities. As the three good monkeys know: close up the doors to perception, ignorance is bliss.

So, in considering the lives of mouths other than one's own, one must be familiar, if not only with the territories of one's own mouth, then also with the supposition that the hungers of other mouths resemble nothing of our own. One must be willing to consider the absence of oneself. To fall in love, and to stay in that free fall for more than the ballyhooed honeymoon period, one must consider appetites that are utterly foreign, become familiar with utter estrangement, be willing, in essence, to forgo the world as we have come to know it, to relinquish basic instinct, common sense.

How can it be, I often marvel, that some people cannot abide chocolate, spinach, coffee, or oysters? Do the sensations of taste — say of an oyster—vary so widely from person to person? Or is it simply (or not so simply) that each taster's associations alter the meaning of such sensations, thereby rendering them more or less distasteful?

When our Irish neighbors visited New York City—years after that supper around our oak plank table—my excitement to share with them the delights of a pot sticker, a piece of sushi—even a coq au vin—defined a widening cultural threshold they had neither the curiosity nor the inclination to cross. They found such hungers, I think, somewhat barbaric, even unhealthy. "Look," I said, pointing to a smoked duck hanging in a Chinatown window, "Doesn't that look *good*?" at which they curled their upper lips, like dogs defending their tried-and-true territory—or more likely, like dogs sensing that this human and Sino-phile appetite might just as well include them on a menu. Such snarling said, "Keep your shaggin' duck to yourself."

My hungers, which do not include an appetite for dogs, insects, nor rodents, would seem finicky in the extreme to most of the world's more omnivorous population. Mostly, that I have never once been truly hungry is perhaps the one thing about me that is most distinctly strange, never mind my flat California drawl. Most human beings have experienced hunger, and many have died from it. When I say I was hungry, I might have also have said, *I really had quite an appetite.* I use the word hunger, as most of us First Worlders do, vocabulary from a life lived according to sublimated and refined desires. What, I wonder, is real hunger?

* * *

I like to go to the Seanache, an old thatched pub about an hour's drive from our neighborhood. Its crooked and dusty floor, white-washed exterior, and huge open fireplace are faithful to the vernacular of the last three centuries. I go there to lap up potato leek soup, to chew good brown bread and watch the coals glow in the open fire.

On a recent visit to the Seanache I notice a sign on the road that reads Famine Graveyard>. A national monument, it turns out, is around the corner from the pub, behind an unassuming and decrepit iron gate. No one is in attendance. It's a simple field, without gravestones, a memorial to the million or more who perished in the notorious Potato Famine of the mid-nineteenth century. Hardest hit, of course, were the anonymous poor, some of whom died where they collapsed, or some who, out of shame, blockaded themselves inside their homes to conceal their wasting.

There had been other famines and periods of hunger in Ireland before, but none to erase a third of its population, none quite like this. This bit of business would stay in the cultural memory for generations:

—*Disease and death in every quarter—the once hardy population worn away to emaciated skeletons—fever, dropsy, diarrhea, and famine rioting*

in every filthy hovel—death diminishing the destitution—hundreds fran-
tically rushing from their home and country, not with the idea of making
fortunes in other lands, but to fly from a scene of suffering and death—
four hundred men starving in one district, having no employment, and
three hundred more turned off the public works in another district, on a
day's notice—seventy-five tenants ejected here, and a whole village in the
last stage of destitution there—Relief Committees threatening to throw
up their mockery of an office, in utter despair—dead bodies of children
flung into holes hastily scratched in the earth, without a shroud or
coffin—wives travelling ten miles to beg the charity of a coffin for a dead
husband, and bearing it back that weary distance—a government offi-
cial offering the one-tenth of a sufficient supply of food at famine
prices—every field becoming a grave, and the land a wilderness!
—A report from the town of Skibbereen, 1846, the *Cork Reporter.*

It is March in the third millennium and where I stand the grass
of the graveyard is wet and new and active with snails. Some set
about the business of finding one another and mating, others
remain at the borders, feasting on the hedge. As I gaze out over the
hedge, dairy cows low and waddle, nearly tripping over their own
udders, and beyond them, fields of barley and wheat roll out
toward the teeming sea. Only a few generations ago this land was
undone, emptied, fallow, denuded. Hunger unraveled families and
those able to remain in their homes were forced to sell their
belongings for a loaf of bread or to burn the lot for fuel.

An outsider might have witnessed the mouths of the fortunate
turned hard against the devastation, baring up the uneasy task of

survivorship, while all around them the lips of the desperate were stained green from eating grass.

* * *

For a simple, perfected ingress—there are mouths that are designed completely for ingestion; the mouths of leeches, of mosquitoes, of the Great Whites. There are the exalted doorways, vaults that yield to "Open Sesame!," bays that open up their Golden Gates, the streaming corridors of Ellis Island, or the gaping sky-lorn maws of the SETI. Bring me your poor, your juicy, your alien harps, your what-have-yous, I'll drink them all in. There is always welcome and danger, and sometimes it can be difficult to discern the difference.

Then for the passage of egress—the bell of the tuba, the rectum of the earthworm, the one-way route of the toothpaste tube. There are mouths customized for transmission of sound, most notably Ethel Merman's, Maria Callas's, or Joe E. Brown's. For content, there's Cassandra, Nostrodamus, or the latest Wall Street pundit. We have babes and horses to broadcast the surest and simplest of truths. And stool pigeons like Sammy "The Bull" Graviano to deliver the inside dope.

There are spewings that are violent, rending. The muzzle of a gun. The mouths of Vesuvius or Krakatoa, or those whose thunder we can only imagine as we peer through a telescope at, say, Europa's effusive calderas. People knock the wind out of us simply by mouthing off, or like Judas, betray first by telling, then by kissing. Boys strike a tough-guy pose and spit as easily—they would have us believe—as shooting their wads; but how different it is to be seen drooling, to be caught in the act of surrogate incontinence.

Which brings us to portals that are decidedly inelegant, which seem to have no purpose or design. The grinning mouths of serendipity, of ramble and meander; or the weak mouths of leakage, of spillage, of the tattling and telltale. There are also mouths whose hungers will not be sated. Envy's ravenous gripe, for one. Try throwing a sop to jealousy, see if it does anything to avert the ferocity, see if you lose your hand to its bottomless appetites. Or try stirring something substantial into the vortex of depression. It will always remain a thin broth, no nutrition. Nothing you add will ever be enough.

Sometimes it seems as though the world is slipping away through these bungholes. There is confusion at the borders, molecules of gold osmose to those of lead, viruses penetrate the cellular wall. Transgressions accrue for no good reason, we trespass as a reflex against those who would trespass against us. Where is the design in that, pray tell? We open ourselves to degeneration, moreover we invite it in.

What is it inside us that welcomes dark angels? For what reason does death confound justice, and come to visit us always too soon? Why can't we cordon ourselves off from harm, batten down the hatches, seal ourselves in a bubble?

As any mouth might eject or blow, hack or keck, spit or spew, one's exit might also serve as someone else's entrance. My love's lips, for example, are also the object of my devotion and therefore the gateway for my departure. The mouths of others can become the ciphers of our souls—not only because they call to us—but because we are eager to exit our skins, our selves, our self-made days. We want to crawl inside the refuge of an other. To molt, become larger, risk leaving the old self behind, become, like Sir Francis Drake at the mouth of the San Francisco Bay, an adventurer.

And so there are mouths simply meant to imagine such journeying, mouths meant to hold our attention, bookmark our ambitions, rend the image of lust indelible. These mouths are iconoclastic. Marilyn's is in perpetual kissablity—continually in the past perfect gerund of perpetual parting, of eternal yielding. And Elvis's, also bee-stung, but cockeyed (is it curled in an insouciant sneer of cool? Or the feral snarl of lust?) both menaces and begs approach, thereby fixing us in its hook.

The other's mouth is the word of our most trusted friend, our beloved's gaze, a policeman's nostrils, the ear of the dog. We enter each and are instantly broken down into someone else's neurons, some other bloke's sensitivities, associations, pathologies; deconstructed according to some joker's values. We become less of ourselves. We are disseminated in much the same way our bones decompose. The ego and its many edifices crumble. What exists in that dark compost of the nonself is a mystery: both terrifying and seductive. Roll me over in the clover. Roll me over, right now.

The mouths of Tragedy and Comedy both share the same

shadowy depth. The earth vents steam and gas. We know the significance without understanding its meaning: Our minds fly as a reflex into the dilating pupil, slick embrace of the vagina, muddy gape of the delta, moss-hewn grotto, wet lip at the well, seal of the crypt, daytime pitch of the mine, well-trod dirt of the lair, musky burrow, magician's hat, bone's socket. We must persist to the very bottom of every quandary, find the light at the end of the tunnel. We are spelunkers, worms, serpents in the gardens of our paradise. What eludes us, seduces us, irritates us, confounds us, calls.

Here I am, a sentient, animate, skirt of meat. Eat me like a steak, like a lover, like a book. See Me, barks the ego. Subsume me, says the soul. Take of this, eat. Destroy, Chew, Digest, Love.

* * *

Bill has given us a bunch of venison. He shot the beast in September, bled and butchered it, then froze the cuts in his freezer. We spend most of the day thawing our piece, then strategizing how to cook it.

Three hours later it is delicious, dark, and musky. The Frankatelli sauce—a name which we repeat to each other out of the sides of our mouths like Chicago gangsters—is sweet and tangy and is a perfect high-frequency foil for the deep registers of this meat. I am enjoying it, but clearly not as much as Rose is. I wonder, does it taste differently to her? What is going on inside that beautiful mouth? What is going on in her innermost, primitive, preproto gut? She says she feels she is "living off the land," so that has enhanced her sense of taste, and satisfaction, and even probably, her nourishment. Her appetite is now like I've never seen it. She is usually able to multi-task, to do several things at once, but here, at this very moment, she is living like a laser beam, like a weasel, focussed on the singular task of pure animal predation. Oh, how I want to enter into each of her orifices, especially right now, her eyes.

How can I know her? She is strange, from another world, by way of a whole different narrative. It is difficult for me to acknowledge and celebrate her hungers—oral, sexual, spiritual—which I may neither share, nor understand. I try to keep curiosity for her alive, though such adventuresomeness feels sometimes like a trip to the dentist for a root canal. And what is the alternative?

The odd thing about mouths is that while I see her, taste her, know her—in so loving—she becomes distinctively more alien; we grow more separate. Which is also, in the zen-like irony of love, how it is that we are becoming intimate. I watch the candlelight gleam from the grease on her chin. Her eyelids close. Her lips flex and glisten like the muscular skin of a stream. She is in heaven, and so, by the grace of my hunger for her, which lives at the mouth of my soul, am I.

* * *

Down into the whirl of its delirium, to the river Lethe, to the river of Woe, down through the esophagus to the belly of the whale, on we go, in we slip. Our bitty cars launch into the tunnel of love, Euridice turns her doubtful eyes to meet ours, and there we are, trapped in the labyrinth. We are drawn to the other's mouths like water to the downspout.

We are, as in our stories of ourselves, on a journey, if not from one carbon incarnation into another, then like a congregation of Horton's Whos, en masse, our galaxy careening toward the Great Attractor. We yearn to be swallowed whole, to become a morsel on the plate of you know Who.

Physicists tell us there are such portals—real live ones, not just the metaphoric variety—tears in the scrim of our everyday. We can, apparently, fall through these holes as a weevil might slip from one end of Swiss to another. Perhaps after being swallowed by such a hole, after being digested in Time's mysterious bowel, we'd emerge at Lourdes or Roswell, where our fans have been gathering, waiting for us to appear, assuming us to be visitors from heaven or Mars.

Look: I approach the Creature, She slows and turns so that her unblinking eye is level with mine. Is it glittering? Can I assume this is a green light? A "come hither." She is making sounds, something like the song of a whale, and a moist tentacle curls around my ear, another up into my nostril. I am being pulled forward, closer, and feel this as the prelude to a kiss. But where do I place my lips? My tongue? All is darkness, humidity, an equatorial ocean. I feel pleasure . . . but it is hers or mine? Perhaps I am inside her already? What sea is this, who is whose Jonah?

Keeping in mind the Hindus:

I (whatever that is), love (whatever that is), you (whatever that is). Oh, it does my heart glad to see you chew, to watch your oil-wet lips roll, to see your nostrils flare as you fill your lungs and sigh with satisfaction, to watch you swallow and smile.

raptures

All things counter, original, spare, strange
Whatever is fickle, freckled (who knows how?)
With swift, slow; sweet, sour; adazzle, dim;
He fathers-forth whose beauty is past change:
Praise him.
—Gerald Manley Hopkins, *Pied Beauty*

It's quiet or it's mad,
It's a good thing, or it's bad
. . . But beautiful, . . . beautiful
—Johnny Burke and Jimmy Van Heusen, *But Beautiful*

*I*magine digging in the dirt with Noah, a three-year-old. You examine each trowel-full, picking clumps out of the scoop and breaking them apart with your fingers. A worm raises its head to the two of you, obscenely moist and pink, it scales the air before stitching itself back into the dirt. Black slugs the size of apple seeds wriggle out of the clay and stick to your fingers like beads of phlegm.

"Yuk," Noah asserts, his pronouncement aimed at your approval, intended to conform to proper sensibilities. Nevertheless, his gaze is locked on these snots, his breathing shallow, and drool collects on his lower lip.

"Yuk," he incants after a moment, though with less conviction.

His eyes veer to yours momentarily, his face telegraphing one question, "Is this ok?" He's too impatient to wait for your answer, his stare tugged back to his trove. Enchantment commands him, won't permit him to toss these nasties. He is now related to them. His fascination, while at first purulent, scatological, is fast approaching love. Noah is starting to look for faces in these aliens. He is exercising his aesthetic muscle, his willingness to suspend prejudice, to question his assumptions about the world.

And just supposing this same eagerness had led him to a scorpion, a wasp, a toadstool?

How necessary are our repulsions; and equally how necessary the inclination to resist them. We are compelled, in spite of what we've been cautioned against, to see the world from all—especially precarious—angles.

High on a mountaintop, in say, the Himalayas, naked fakirs are cross-legged in the snow, eyes rolled back, oblivious to the cold.

Meanwhile, 130 feet below the sea off the island of Catalina, a diver has sunk into another kind of rapture. An excess of nitrogen in his blood steeps him in the realm of the gorgeous. The sea is awash with siren's song. It will be the most beautiful thing he had ever experienced.

Susceptibility to the sublime can be at odds with survival, safety, common sense. Mirage has the power to lull us into ecstatic peril, can cause us to linger in the bull's-eye, loiter in the beams of an oncoming truck.

And what if—cautions the voice of the safely monochromatic— love is such lethal fancy?

Nevertheless, in experiment after experiment the scientist exposes herself to radiation, the vulcanologist stays too long at the lip of the caldera, the virgin's palms split open and bleed, the lover endures the impossible trials of loving. In every memorable tale, the hero places herself at risk. And for what?

A face, a gaze, the curve of a mouth, the slope of a brow? A Pythagorean proof, perhaps, the diatonic scale, a rhyme, a nude, a myth, a bauble, a sunset, Venus Di Milo, Miss America, a vintage Burgundy, a bed of roses, prime numbers, the double helix, damask linen, a unified field theory, Sophia Loren? This rapture, this calamity, this divinity is vain, and she walks in it like the night, and truth is it, and it is a joy forever. It is in the eye of the beholder, and it is as it does.

* * *

Long, long ago, an old merchant was returning home from a fair in winter. The distance had been far and he was cold and tired. He longed to be back in his house with his three daughters, seated before his hearth, safe and warm. Before leaving them he had asked each what to bring her as a gift from his journey. And so, as requested, he purchased a topaz ring for the oldest daughter, an emerald necklace for the second, but nothing, yet, for his favorite—who, in characteristic modesty, had asked for nothing. She was kind and comely, and never asked anything of him, never even for the smallest of souvenirs.

All night the old man rode his tall white horse through the snow, troubled to be returning to his favorite child empty-handed. "What to give her?" the horse hooves whispered, "What to give her. . . . "

By dawn he woke to find his horse had led him to a splendored garden, leafed and lavish, even in the frost. Beyond the perimeter of the garden the trees and bushes were bare; but inside greenery flourished. And then something caught his eye, a rose trailing along the garden wall, bright as a gemstone.

Never had he seen such a splendid flower! A gift for Beauty, he thought. At last, something for Beauty! He dismounted his mare and cut the rose from the briar, but as he did he heard a voice thunder from behind the topiary, "Give me back my rose, or I'll kill you!"

The old man leapt on his horse and they fled, and they were nearly home when he heard something loping and panting beside him. Turning around, he saw a horrid Beast that cried out, "Give me back my rose, or I'll kill you!"

The horse was exhausted and in a lather. The man despaired: he begged, "Please let me keep it. I am supposed to bring a gift to my daughter . . . the most beautiful child in all the world."

"Fine! Well, since you have plundered my garden, give me your beautiful daughter for a wife!"

And so it happened that Beauty—the most lovely of women, the old man's dearest child—was taken away by the Beast.

Beauty is an odd name for a girl isn't it? Beauty. We have Charity, Prudence, Grace, Hope, a slew of almighty virtues to name the baby, but never something as audacious as Beauty. It would be a curse, wouldn't it? When she was born she was luminous, and even as toddler she dazzled. Too bad she didn't know it. Oh, you could attribute her lack of self-esteem to the way her jealous sisters treated her, acting like she was their scullery maid, as they adorned their bodies with perfumes and jewels, as they rubbed her nose in the muck of their envy. Such comeliness, as it turns out, has its price.

What would it be like to become Beauty? To be the shiny coin passed from hand to hand, the lucre we live by, the gelt that is, like it or not, the measure of our wealth, our ambition, our poverty. We may scorn and squander it, but where would we be without its dominion? What captures us time after time? What other god, besides fear, do we serve?

* * *

Good art, dutiful art, art that redeems the world, appears at first ugly, inappropriate. It is the mutant creature crawling up onto the land, the opposable thumb, the sixth finger, the third eye. By necessity it must focus on the wrong subject matter, champion the worst imaginable faux pas, applaud the vulgarian's bark. It is Costello to Abbott, Ralph to Alice, Beast to Beauty, a whoopee cushion at a formal dinner party. It will make us either guffaw, snort, gag or weep. It refreshes wonder. It says, "Look," and "Look again."

If art can impose upon us the stun of rapture, if it is the antidote for boredom, the dispeller of hubris, the finder of lost articles, the foe of even repulsion, then it is the soul's daily bread. And it is also, incidentally, love's identical work. All it takes is a kiss to turn the toad, the gnome, the Beast into a prince.

Recently the Detroit police raided an art exhibit accompanying a conference on censorship. One of the pieces considered obscene and confiscated in the raid was a reproduction of a painting called *The Origin Of The World*. There's no doubt the work intended to rile the staus quo, even if that initial establishment was the French art world of 1866. *The Origin Of The World* is, as it was then, a beaver shot. The painting's maker, Gustave Courbet, had made a name for himself by choosing callow, lowbrow subject matter to ennoble in the context of "Art."

Let's go back to the dirt where the child, Noah, and you were digging for buried—and now newly realized—treasure. It is Rose's dirt. Rose's garden, the garden in which Rose grows roses. It is the same dirt in which Rose and I discovered a common ground in beauty, in which, still strangers, we ate breakfast together at her patio table, and watched as a snail slid on the underbelly of glass, beneath the pastries, the napkins, and the champagne flutes. Our conversation stopped and we watched how the muscle of the snail's belly rippled as she glided, how her motility was reminiscent of an ancestry in the sea. When she reached the edge she righted herself atop, her brown shell as domed as a walnut's, and proceeded to coast toward what was left of my croissant. We watched her lift her head to the golden crumb, and we hushed and both swore we could hear the soft sound of something tearing. We named her Carla. "She's beautiful!" Rose exclaimed. "Yes," I agreed, one of the loveliest creatures I'd ever seen.

There are times when the gods appear to us in the guises of animals or beautiful mortals. Such trickery could be the first step down the slippery slope, the bait at death's door. Think of all the dupes of wicked mermaids, sailors lost to a watery grave. Imagine yourself gaily stumbling down the alleys of Hamlin, traipsing after a piper's ditty. Rapture is heaven's ruse to engage us in conversation, otherwise we are too oblivious (or too cowed) to engage on our own. We are Beauty's hostage, and how or where she finds us will either bring about our ruin or our salvation.

There are some tricks with this painting of a woman's crotch, with *The Origin Of The World*. The first is the pairing of the title with the image, a proclamation that the universe owes its genesis in a female body, a female being. We've seen Venuses depicted before throughout the course of western Art History, with Neolithic stone carvings blossoming into classic marbles; and even in Courbet's time, rouged courtly ladies romped through scenes from classic mythology. Courbet's subject however, sprawling lasciviously on a background of tousled bed linens, hardly cuts an Olympian figure. Courbet's irreverent deification of the Female, while by definition wholly classical, expands the frame in which Beauty can be beheld. Here, flesh and blood women, freshly fucked women are the proper, indeed the essential, subject matter. "Show me an angel," claimed Courbet, "and I'll paint one."

The second trick, also a pun on classicism, is to lop off parts of the figure: the limbs and the head. Think of the *Venus Di Milo* or *The Winged Victory* and there you have our nineteenth century demoiselle, her extremities cropped by the artist's perspective. Such amputations, while playing with the aesthetics of classicism, also give his subject two wholly opposing attributes. Without features or identity this very mortal harlot becomes not simply a female, but Female, an archetype. God, Courbet might have said, is secular.

The darkness of the pubis is equal to the infinite dark beyond the bed folds, an unreal blackness, as quixotic as the starry sky. The folds of the drapery mirror the folds of the figure, and into both depths the eye wants to slip, toward mystery, toward intimacy. One has the feeling that it would be easy to slip one's hand, one's gaze, into those pockets, to finger the stuff of which we're all made.

Don't get me wrong, I don't think Courbet was a great painter. But he was a champion, perhaps one of the first, of the avant-garde, one of the first transgressives. Someone who, like Warhol with his soup cans, said, "Look." "Even Here." And like most artists, he was reputed to be something of an egomaniac—hardly someone who was able to live by his own creed.

Love and Art are bigger than we are, and a great deal more interesting. There is no celebrity in either. Meet your favorite author and you quickly experience the discrepancy between those labyrinthine sentences and their pimply, vain, maker. Likewise, once you know your love, she's no longer Ava Gardner. Yet, in love—say, in looking together at a snail or a soup can—you are both in Grace.

The poet Robert Pinsky says that the artist's job is to make poems where none has been before. To make some aspect of living poetic, the way the city was made poetic by Dickens, the way that perhaps the city had never been poetic before Dickens. Why do we crave such poetics? Isn't life just ducky as is? Apparently not. Apparently our need to salvage our lives through finding beauty in them is as important, as inseparable, as living them. This is why, in William Carlos William's words concerning poetry, "people die each day for lack of it."

* * *

Hardly purgatory, the Beast's castle was a step up from her family home. The garden in perpetual bloom, animate statuary proffering candelabras, and musicians vamping round the clock. Food of every description appeared even before Beauty knew she had an appetite. Her wardrobe was brimming with silks and cashmeres, and her bed linens unfurled for her if she even started to yawn.

She enjoyed the luxury, but more than that she had begun to take interest in her fiancé. She liked his kind, submissive gaze, and the way his tale swung slow and low to the ground, whisking up small clouds of dust whenever he stood before her. She was amused by his anxious growl at the voices on the other side of the garden wall. And she was endeared to him especially when he pleaded with her to remove burrs from the inside of his paws or from the back of his ears. She was beginning, in fact, to enjoy that smell.

But one day she said to him, "I worry that my father is sick. Please allow me to return home to see him."

The Beast was afraid to let her go, but he gave in. He was becoming a bit of a slave. As she was leaving, he called out, "Don't stay long, or I, too will take ill." Then he growled in the direction of her departure, and slunk back inside the gate, and trotted up to his study.

When she arrived home her father had died. She stayed for the funeral, the dinner, and the funeral reception. She cared for her vain sisters and cleaned the house and even wrote the obit for the local paper. But she was a Queen now, or about to be, and something inside her had changed. Her sisters saw it, too. She was more substantial, not to be toyed with. So there was no stopping her when she announced "I must get back to my beau."

When she returned she found her castle dark and chill. It was as though Persephone herself had been gone. Snow was everywhere; frost starched the drapery, and icicles dangled from the faucets. Not one note of music could be heard in any chamber, just her own voice calling for her mate, and the wind whining through the rafters.

Outside in the garden the roses were wilted and brown. She pushed them aside and found her Beast, dying in the cold.

She took his great head in her lap and cried, " Oh, my King, I can't live without you!" Her tears fell, one by one into his mouth, and slowly he licked his lips, and blinked his eyes, and smiled. The rest is mythic history.

* * *

There is another kind of art. Harder, less dramatic.

One can look at *The Origin Of The World* and have one's vision of the Feminine refreshed. One might even assume that one could even paint such a comparable painting. It is quite another thing to live with such values. Is your lover a goddess? Can you bring such poetics, such creative effort, to your everyday life? Can you live with the knowledge of your exquisite, and very ordinary, mortality?

It is one thing to rescue the outcast, the forsaken, the downright Beastly—that gets the hero's reception, the ticker tape parade down main street, a throne at Olympus, a role in a fairy tale—or at the very least a child's awe, a gasp of amazement. To champion the mundane is quite another matter. It is quiet, daily effort, requiring Sisyphian ingenuity. Like the chores of housewifery, one must set the table, light the candles, say the prayers. Love, if it is to be sustained, and if it survives the dissipation of the ideal, requires such endurance, such stubborn genius.

We struggle in life against both familiarity and detachment, and the shadows of contempt that lie everywhere in between. We sweat to keep our gaze fresh, to lasso amazement, even when the sink is filled with dirty dishes, and the sky has been overcast for weeks.

Look at Beauty's life after marrying the Beast, after he becomes a prince: it is hardly happily-ever-after. She misses his whiskers, his feral breath, his scrappy, jagged nails. What has rescued Beauty, made her real, sanctified her, is her concupiscence with the ugliest cuss in sight. She became soiled, surrendered idealization. But once everything is prettified, where's the rub? What can rise to the occasion of beauty?

Besides, life is long and beauty fades. What kind of castle looms for lovers doomed to the lifelong haul?

The saying goes that beauty is as beauty does. Could that mean that

to confer beauty unto something or someone, to discover something otherwise forsaken, is to become beautiful? And moreover, not to do it just
once—that would be easy, as easy as kissing a frog—but to continually
salvage love from the brutal revelations of intimacy, ah, that would take
some enchantment!

So by night they have to remember themselves, become grotesques,
accept the natures they were given; so by morning they are redeemed in
the eyes of the other. They scream and fight sometimes with words not
befitting a fairy tale. They have to light their own candelabras, and sing
their corny off-key songs, and force themselves to journey away from each
other. Their fangs are sharp, their glamour for their eyes alone, and they
manage each day to maintain the holy trance.

* * *

Put simply, she was beautiful. She was cradling her infant, and she
was radiant. She was staring off into the distance, a kind of heroic
pose, her black eyes shining, her facial muscles relaxed. I beheld her,
by which I mean, I drank in her beauty, this mother gorilla at the
Seattle Zoo. As a reflex I turned to the stranger beside me. "She's really
beautiful!" I gaped. It was a moment like Noah's, in which I had lost
propriety, coordinates, my frame of reference. Could this be real? Was
I in the presence of a simian Sophia Loren? The stranger, a zoo official, eyed me. "Yes," she began cautiously, "she is . . . *very.*" Her resistance to my blurt was not only proprietary, she was defensive. This
was the kind of revelation one doesn't share freely. There are places
for people who's tastes veer toward the . . . unconventional.

This was the same week that a woman schoolteacher in Seattle was arrested for having an affair with her eleven-year-old student. He was beautiful to her, more mature, more understanding than most males even her own age. She was convinced, though at times guilt-ridden, that this boy was exceptional. Was she in a trance? Or was she finally awake?

This was same month I realized I was smitten by Eamonn, my ten-year-old neighbor in Ireland. I did not want to have sex with this child, but I admired his beauty, his charm, his spirit, and there was an erotic aspect to it. I loved his boyness, his emerging masculinity and I felt our connection to be deep and mysterious. I called it a crush, and knew it to be mutual.

That was the same year that Rose and I built the addition onto our cottage.

After we rolled the second coat of paint over the plaster, a snail slid onto the windowsill of what was to become our kitchen, our first overnight guest. She was flatter, more elliptical than our Carla, her yellow-banded spiral like a hypnotist's whirligig. Rose held out her finger to her and waited. She was shyer than our Carla, slower to emerge. First came her clitoral head, then her sprocket eyes. One fixed on Rose, the other aimed at me. Below them, her olfactory sensors, the smaller pair of eye-like sprockets, touched the skin on Rose's finger tentatively, then retreated, then reached out again.

And then she tasted Rose. Like a spring percolating through muddy water, or a small cloud gathering in a dark sky, her mouth materialized out of her dim flesh, and puckered on Rose's skin. Rose exclaimed her excitement with an intake of breath, then laughed, said the snail's mouth was like the mouth on the puppet "Lambchop."

This made me love Rose all the more, made me want to ravish her there amid the rubble of our new kitchen. This kitchen which would in time feed our neighbors, in which lamb would be broiled and roasted and stewed, in which tables would be set with linens and silver, and flowers placed in vases, and candles lit. This is the kitchen in which fangs would be bared and hair would fly, in which tears would be shed, and vows rescinded, and threats leveled, and love forsaken. The place where rapture would then be recaptured. The dirt where beauty is found.

dust

n the opening of the film *2001*, a freshly gnawed bone is flung skyward by a clever hominid and—in one simple splice—evolves into a spaceship soaring toward an uncertain destiny. The enigma of Stanley Kubrick's most famous movie matched the mystery of human life here on our singular mote in the Milky Way. What is our destination, is it toward our maker, ourselves, toward some burgeoning revision of being Human? For decades after the movie was released, *2001* became a synonym for our fear of The Future. It was an allusion to our growing angst about modernization, cold-hearted technology, and loss of human values.

Now of course, having been lived, the year 2001 conjures different scenes, most indelibly of pulverized skyscrapers and desert bunkers; images having less to do with intergalactic travel and promethean technology, and more with cities and villages laid to waste, once again, by human conflict; images, in short, not unlike those found in the ancient texts of the Bible, the Koran, the Bhagavad-Gita . . .

In 2001, on a terrestrial autumn morning, millions of people everywhere on this planet were witness to the same set of pictures, the same story as it unfolded, live, on television. I was two hours from the scene, in Long Island New York. I went to the TV, pressed the remote and watched as the light flickered onto the screen, dawning into an implausible image. Smoke hurled out of one of the ugly towers I knew to be the World Trade Center. Like the smoke rings I can fashion out of the O of my mouth, this torrent held the shape of a plane in the exit wound of Tower One.

Within minutes that shot was upstaged by another. A new plane careered into the picture . . . and all apertures were open. We, by which I mean the bystanders, the amateur photographers, the camera crews, the entire television audience at this point, those of us gawking in our pajamas gripping a remote, we were all poised, mouths agape, pupils dilated, no missing the moment. We were stooges, set up for the punch line, the sight gag, the whammy.

My take, the one I will carry as The Icon, was the one on ABC. From this angle the plane entered the right side of the frame, cut an exquisite curve in the bright fall sky, heading dead-on into the back of the tower's twin, right hook, no mistaking the bull's-eye, bursting ablaze into the foreground.

So after the stun of it, the tarried, delayed, languorous sludge of refusal and acceptance, after this second plane impacted the second tower and its meaning was beginning, slowly, to form, the ongoing spectacle started to torque. Images linked to other images; a montage was strung, a rosary of cinematic clauses.

Horror, and—shall I be flogged for such admission?—excitement to ride its acceleration. Could I see that hit again, a few hundred times? Yes, oh yes, I had to. And did I, as we all did, incredulous, from every angle imaginable.

These perpetrators, "terrorists" they were already being referred to in the media—whatever enmity they felt for us—had such an understanding, such a feel for (would here substitute L-O-V-E for) our construction of and devotion to imagery. It would necessarily follow that only desire could fashion such spite.

* * *

Looking back, this moment unfolds in slow-motion. For me it's how it actually happened. When my brothers came to my high school to tell me my father had died, I saw them move toward me like divers trudging across the ocean floor. This is how the event is etched into the record of my experience. Absolute reality, you cannot argue me otherwise. Slo-mo is the axis upon which I can rotate the monstrosity, try to familiarize myself with it, revisit my lack of comprehension.

Something, not just the workings of memory, but our juggle with disbelief alters time, our experience of the moment. Horror roars headlong toward us, and in the compromise between perception and reorganization, some doppler effect floods our neurons, leaves us ogling its wake.

Often our impressions of catastrophe, however inaccurate, are more dazzling than the facts. Scientists now studying this phenomenon call it "flashbulbing" and predict that many of us will swear we witnessed the impact of the towers as they occurred in real time, rather than later, in replay, as most certainly most of us did. The spectacle of trauma, they suggest, often displaces the real.

How do we organize our memory of disaster? Are traumatic events captured with the exactitude of a camera; or are they simply exacted by a fiction, fixed forever *as though* in a photograph? How do we chronicle life, all the while experiencing it?

And how did we conceive of these imprints of memory, the monumentalizing of experience, before the advent of the photograph and the moving picture? There is something about our knowledge of slow-motion photography, of flashbulbing and freeze-framing, of fast-forwarding and rewinding, of cutting and splicing that has given us both a map and a lexicon for perception.

In art, as in trauma, an event is hoisted to the pitch of an Event. Both vie for the same ends: to fix time, to organize experience, to domesticate its nature. From the muck of existence we strive to fashion our little stories, mold our iconography, and shift the tense in which we live to the archetypal *past perfect*. In our struggle to tame life, to soften its ferocity, we miss most of it. Where did it go as we reworked the plot, as we edited one more version?

* * *

Americans are zealots for imagery. It is our free market export, our cash crop, our bread and butter; but it is also our Frankenstein, the invention now run amok, the gears upon which, like Chaplin, we find ourselves caught. Are we free? We buy merchandise, even masturbate according to its dazzle. We can barely experience a vista without a camera to memorialize it for us. Some would say the picture has replaced the vista. Others would say each picture robs its subject of its soul. Still others might conclude each picture, lit up with bells and whistles, each blinking and chiming like a Vegas slot machine, makes us its slave, robs us of our souls.

One can put too much faith in pictures. Or said differently, such reality as one finds in an image is not more valuable than what you may grasp blindly, casting about in a clutter of unknown quantities. Think of the big moments in life, the ones that won't fit themselves into the frame: someone you thought you couldn't live without leaves, someone disappoints, you find you are fallible. A lifetime will be spent forging Sense from the spark of being stunned. Then what happens? You're on a gurney gasping for breath, or on a cell phone in a building about to crumble. . . . Forget your ornate stories. It can get very simple then: first person pronoun, verb, second person familiar. Forget the words "as" or "like." All is short, declarative, unambiguous. What could all our iconography amount to compared to a pile of our floury remains?

There is wisdom in a culture that would caution us against graven images. Of course what do we, by whom I now mean Westerners, notably Americans, know of such cultures? Only caricatures: seductive sheiks, amorous belly dancers, fundamentalist crazies, titillation to mask the ignorance brought about by our own brand of cultural fanaticism.

Why do we sensationalize, often sexualize, that mysterious frontier? Perhaps desire provides the frame in which mysteries may appear familiar, supple, even within our budget. Wanting is not only the bee in our enterprising bonnet, the honey in our compulsive hive, it becomes our surrogate Queen, our escape from the pressing void, the tune we whistle in the dark.

Maybe, for lack of conviction, we cling to celebrity and spectacle, to the glamour and traffic of representations. Maybe for lack of purpose we escape to the safe haven of desire, where we can stroke ourselves, and reexperience the surety that all our fascinations are fundamental.

Likewise, mightn't They, our New Enemies, inhabitants of this murky frontier, mightn't They also be trying to escape? To run from desire by fleeing to the paradise of the nobler, the safer; to dazzle themselves with absolutes, and ward off the gnawing of their own wants? Our kingdom of imagery, replete with conveniences and lifestyles, flesh and fantasy, must seem like Hell indeed. Mightn't They cling to the certainty that faith is fundamental?

Yeats articulated the psychic duality between purpose and passion in *The Second Coming*. He envisioned a "gyre" about to unhinge our times, and at its center a moral vacuum in which, "The best lack all conviction, while the worst/ are full of passionate intensity."

So this is how it has begun to look: us against Them, good versus evil, subject in the foreground, object in the background. Isn't that the way we always see it? Here we both are in a showdown. Rock cave versus skyscraper, Holy versus Infidel, Fundamentalist versus Libertine, religious ideals versus marketable desires.

We peer across the frontier at each other and see the Barbarian staring back. Yet we are each shadows of the other, provide the missing—therefore reviled—piece of the other's soul. (Not unlike LOVE.)

What would happen if we lived our lives with more conviction, or theirs more free?

The feminist Muslim writer, Fatema Mernissi concludes her memoir *Dreams of Trespass* with a story from her childhood, in which she goes to her Sudanese servant and asks why there should be a separation between boys and girls. Mina explains,

> ". . . *whenever there is a frontier, there are two kinds of creatures walking on Allah's earth, the powerful on one side, and the powerless on the other.*"
> *I asked Mina how I would know on which side I stood. Her answer was quick, short and very clear: "If you can't get out, you are on the powerless side."*

From Whom does such power come? (Trick question.)

Who are "They," and who are "We?" What do we each possess to make the other complete? How do we step out onto our frontiers, keeping both desire and devotion as points on our compass?

* * *

On the morning of September 12th, I drove into Manhattan. The

Long Island Expressway was empty of traffic except for the rush of police and fire trucks streaming in from elsewhere in the state. I heard on the radio that a shop in Long Island, owned by a Muslim, had been vandalized. The reflex of retribution had begun.

Miles before I could spot the top of the Empire State Building, the default harbinger of the new city, I could both smell and see the cloud. It hovered, less like the fiend I had seen the night before on television, more like a wraith.

The cloud and its special weather, like the inside of a storm, was something we had discovered through a lens, but something only rescue workers, or the media could enter and experience firsthand. There was all that was outside of the cloud, distinct from the horror, the rest of Manhattan breathing under another sparkling fall day. Yet even this distinction hardly spared anyone from the smell. The reek of scorched plastic and pulverized cement, the funk of smelter and incinerated flesh was prevalent no matter where you were.

I found a parking lot near a barricade on Fourteenth Street and made my way on foot toward the place where Rose was. All traffic below Fourteenth was stopped, and this new pedestrian neighborhood of confused, solemn, but determined citizens was the place I needed to be. Even the dogs out on their walks seemed to soldier their jobs more resolutely, bearing the deeper devotion to a troubled pack.

Survivors were defending themselves the best way they knew how: man on bicycle, woman on Rollerblades, baby in backpack, each with a dust mask.

Grit settled on the windowsills. It was pale and gray and made up of tiny crystals of glass and steel and cement. Asbestos fibers, no doubt, lay unseen, as well as unknown compounds forged by the concussions. The fouled air hung in the sky for months.

* * *

By mid-October they reopened the Chambers Street station, the closest subway stop that hadn't been destroyed. I got up before dawn and took the subway down, hoping to beat the inevitable flood of looky-loos like me.

The second the subway doors slid open the assault of ash began, two floors below street level. Whatever it was I hoped to discover in the realms above, it was already upstaged by the stench.

From what I'd seen from TV of the stuff they've barged over to Staten Island, and sorted through, and picked at, and in some cases, typed for DNA, the chaff, minus the metal, looked like the stuff you dig out of the fireplace, the stuff in a cremation box, a lot of Granny's cooled cinders. They say the brave forensic detectives raking through the dregs occasionally found a charred body part or something completely discrete, like a wallet or a ring, but little really remained of the remains.

To me, barricaded from Ground Zero by a few blocks, the mountain known as "The Pile" looked pink and warm. Maybe it's just the primitive desire for a corpse at the crime scene, something appreciable to grieve, but there was something comforting about its bulk. I wanted to get a close-up of that body, to scan its immensity, to stand in the midst of sixteen acres of pulverization and—click—somehow seize its gist.

My mistake, the mistake of all us gawkers squeezed at the barricade, was that no snapshot could conclude the scope of the disaster, nor ease our insecurity. A woman in a jogging suit stood in my sight line, her camera pressed to her face, she moved from side-to-side, bent her knees, stymied by her inability to cram the spectacle into the frame. The best "views" of this crematorium were still from the helicopter shots. But the best insight, perceptible from any vantage, was the one streaming in through our nostrils.

It was everywhere. It was clumped in the planters of thirsty birches and ficus along Broadway. It clung like dirty snow to the awnings above sushi shops and discount clothing stores. It flanneled the windows in the downtown, providing the perfect medium for the graffiti scribblers. Names were scrawled in that powder, each a declaration: "Leon," Bobo," "Billy" . . . who were these immortals? Before that day the area had been labeled a crime scene; no one until that morning was allowed in. Not likely to be the work of local residents or rescue workers, these were the names of the city's invisibles, the lumpen, the forsaken. . . .

I felt the touch of their finger traces, remembered the Neolithic handprints in the caves in Southern France. Some things never change. How intimate to trace your name through the residue of three thousand people. How vulgar, how insignificant, how human! The curvilinear graffiti were already fading as, by the minute, more of the dead settled like sediment at the bottom of the sea.

If there is something positive in the iconography of "The Pile," and all the other images that continued to accrete into this national tragedy, it's the possibility that the mantra of contemporary anxiety "what if" will be replaced by "when." We now know, if briefly, how vulnerable, how mortal, we are. Shit—digital, high resolution, Kodacolor—happened. We once were a nation of isolationists, commitment-phobics; but we now are obliged to confront the Other in all its new guises. It's no longer possible to dream away the vagaries of the third law of thermodynamics. . . . Everything feared is not only probable, but inevitable: No one gets out alive.

If, at long last, we're lucky, we'll show our hand, exhaust our cellular reserves, play full out.

Rose jokes, in her best faux High-Yankee spracht: "we've nothing to fe-yah but fe-yah itself."

What would it be like to confront fear itself? To sidestep the knee jerk, the spasm of defensiveness, the hedge of anxious speculation, and go directly to—against every instinct to do otherwise—the site.

How might it be, FOR EXAMPLE, to survive the wreck of abandonment, betrayal, loss? It's a fate, as the saying goes, worse than death. . . . Otherwise why the continual drama that upstages living? Otherwise why the timidity that keeps us with a toe poised at the rushing water?

Or, FOR ANOTHER EXAMPLE, how would it be to confront *death*? Innocence would drown, no doubt, but life, at last, would be lived.

* * *

There is a painting that hangs in the office of Afghanistan's Foreign

Ministry. It's a picture of the Intercontinental Hotel in Kabul, painted in the 70s, when this once-upon-a-time luxury spot was in its prime. In this painting, the majestic Intercon, built in the international modernist style, sits imperiously on a darkly forested hill, ringed by a drapery of snowy blue mountains.

Nowadays there is no snow, and the fir trees surrounding the faded hotel have been stripped of even their bark. Goats nip the greenery down to the nub; crows peck at whatever seeds are left. Hotel workers, dressed in soiled brown uniforms, break up hotel rubble for a large wood burning stove in the hotel's frigid kitchen. Whatever is left over in the landscape, the stubs of rose bushes and grape vines, the scrub of Mulberry and Juniper trees, are all in such decline, it won't be long before they'll also make their way to the flames. Dust is what's left. The site has been desiccated by draught, and decimated by war. If one were to paint the Intercon and her environs today, from the same vantage, it would be in a monochrome palette of tans and grays.

From my balcony on the fourth floor, dusty and bullet-pocked, I see small dun-colored houses to my left and a huge dusty field to my right. Men stride across that field, often in pairs, their tan woolen blankets clutched tightly around their shoulders. Women traipse along in groups, each sequestered under her burqa, one hand gripping the blue fabric against the wind while the other gesticulates, nudges, fondles. Peace has been in force here for only a few weeks; the Taliban has been overthrown, and the Al Queda, the visiting terrorist network responsible for the attack on my country, have sought refuge in the mountains to the south. Now a few children in this field fly kites, and the sound of popular music, sexy and secular, rises windborne from car stereos.

This is what the epicenter of disaster looks like.

Here is the much-feared site—without the psychological overlay—the actual stone-cold nucleus of devastation. Here a place whose pique of impending catastrophe won't be interrupted by the entrance of a Rod Serling, or the routine chime of an alarm clock. This is not a place of "what ifs."

A few days before the end of 2001, I'd flown into Afghanistan on a UN flight from Pakistan. Rose, who had been writing from the region for months, invited me to join her. "Come," she said, "You must see this place." And so, while peace was in force, at least in Kabul, I decided to seize my opportunity.

My plane, crammed with journalists and aid workers, was also bearing a substantial cargo of California champagne, western booty for the first Christmas at the US Embassy since it was abandoned twelve years ago.

Had anyone asked me, I was prepared to pass myself off as one more of the hundreds of journalists here. But should anyone really notice, they'd have seen I was too green and wide-eyed. I was there simply to ogle history, to witness something important in my lifetime; to get a first hand view into our frontier.

* * *

Our white hatchback, the windshield plastered with a poster of the national hero, Commander Massoud, just blew a tire on the Shomali plain. It's easy to get a flat here, the roads suffer the scars of bombs and missiles, and it's not uncommon to hit a pit in the concrete. A driver must navigate his course by zigzagging from one side of the road to the other. Like most things in Afghanistan, driving is by necessity anarchic. Right of way is Darwinian, negotiated by horn blasts and sheer dare. And also, like most things here, driving requires absolute focus, as dangers present themselves suddenly and from any direction.

I am falling in love with our driver, a young Panjshiri named Najib. Najib who is all of twenty-three years old is considering taking another wife (though he will get hell from his first). I'm in love with his black loafers worn without socks, his long white *shalwar kamiz,* his Northern Alliance scarf that he wears around his head like a sheik, and his purple blazer (with padded shoulders). From the back, with his headscarf and with both hands gripping the wheel, he looks like a nervous Turkish matron. I'm in love with this winning white smile and his red lips. In love with the hand that comes into the car window cupping soft bread piled with freshly grilled lamb. "Gooood! Eat!"

Najib knows this stretch of road; he spent more than a few nights out on the Shomali Plain dodging missiles and mortar fire. He fought for the Northern Alliance under its handsome Commander Massoud.

For miles in every direction mud brick houses are bombed into rubble. Adobe outcroppings, once-upon-a-time villages, are softened by erosion from wind and the occasional rain. Bare trees and acres of withering vineyards surround them. I am feeling a powerful desire to irrigate, even finding myself daydreaming of it. In an inane American fantasy I envision myself standing in the landscape holding a green garden hose. "Can't some of these vineyards be saved?" I ask Faheem, our interpreter. "They are mined," he answers, "No one can tend them. . . . This whole area is mined."

The roadway is littered with the detritus of warfare, with skeletal trucks and tanks, the rusted hulls of downed jetfighters, empty rail road cars, all filigreed with hundreds of bullet holes . . . and graveyards, each marked with a simple stone, some no bigger than a child's head, or with flags of green cloth, the color of the Northern Alliance. And occasionally along this road, rocks are painted yellow or white, and line the gritty shoulder, and signal that mines are just a misstep away.

Before the tire blew we were on our way to the grave of the Lion of Panjshir, the martyr whose craggy, appealing face appears on posters plastered everywhere in this country. Ahmad Shah Massoud. Massoud was murdered two days before the attack on the World Trade Center by two members of the Al Qaeda masquerading as journalists. "These Arabs," Najib queries, in a voice that is now thick with hate, "they also bomb a big house in your country?"

As we stand by the car with its flat tire, . . . and with no jack, Najib spies five old men, bearded, elegant, walking up the highway . . . "Ha! . . . one, two, three, four, . . . five jacks! Ha Ha!" Najib laughs triumphantly, tossing me a smile and showing off his beautiful teeth. Our jacks arrive, lift the car long enough for Najib to slip on the spare. Our jacks drop the car, shoot us curious sidelong glances, nod good day, and continue to walk. Najib tightens the lug nuts. We climb back into the car and I see that he has slung his holster and .38 over the back of his seat. He brushes the grit off his jacket and guns the engine. . . .

Along the way children are filling the craters in the road with dirt, and Najib tosses paper money out the window for them. The bills flutter behind us and the children throw down their shovels and run to clutch them out of the wind. It's the Afghan version of a toll road.

We start our climb into the Panjshir valley, on a dirt road that runs parallel to the river. We enter the portal of a gorge, mountains vault above us, the river slices below. You can feel Najib's excitement as he nears his home. He stops at a small stream trickling snowmelt, cups his hands and drinks the water like a sommelier. "Clean!" He boasts, "MMMM...gooood! Come! Drink!"

The valley is austere and alpine. Orchards of apple and mulberry cut into the foothills and alongside each banked village. Ditches have been engineered to merge the river with the small farms planted with wheat and leeks. Children with dark Keene eyes and chicken pox scars wave to us and yell what every Afghan apparently now knows by heart, "Hello! How are you?" Even a goat steps from a doorway to stare into our car as we pass. It would be sweet, if not for the evidence of warfare at every turn.

Beyond the tidy farmlands, below the silver flux of the river, tanks lay submerged and upended. The implements of war are imbedded in the everyday. Tank treads reinforce the roadbed. Mortar shell casings decorate the tops of walls and window ledges. The valley is home to many Afghan warlords. Dr. Abdullah Abdullah lives in a grand house overlooking the water. And the charismatic freedom fighter, The Lion, once lived just a bouncy jeep ride away.

As we pass the fallen commander's house, Najib clears his throat. "I think," he labors without Faheem's help, "If I see an Arab I will kill him."

We arrive at the newly constructed grave, a wooden pagoda high atop the river, and the wind practically sweeps us off the edge. A helicopter roars above us, adding to the wind flap. Inside the structure freshly cut pine logs brace the walls and joist the tile roof. The floor is dirt and it rises to one massive heap in the center. This grave, planted with grass and flowers, both living and dried, is larger than life, a grave for a god. It must be at least fifteen feet long and four feet high. Men continually fuss over it, whisking it with small brooms, picking dried up pods and fallen petals. Najib caresses the dirt, takes two stalks of purple cockscomb from it, and squats nearby to weep.

When we get back in the car I hand Najib a tissue . . . had he ever seen one? Was this an obscene gesture? I am racked with shame over my culture's petty privileges. He wipes his eyes and blows his nose. His generosity has been remarkable. He's wanted us to taste the flavors of his beloved land, and even now to witness his grief.

"Please," Najib says through Faheem, with characteristic Afghan hospitality, "I would be honored for you to stay at my home in the Panjshir. I would be your servant."

Is there love at the site of devastation?
What's not to love?

* * *

Days later we are on our way to visit the literal Lion of Afghanistan, the surviving lion at the Kabul Zoo. It takes a while to get to this part of town, the streets are bombed out, and our car journeys laterally, right to left and back again, like a duck in a shooting gallery, barely winging the onslaught of craters. This part of Kabul is, inconceivably, more devastated. It is the urban version of what I saw on the Shomali plain, utter ruin. People walk into, and through their houses simply by stepping over rubble that once was wall. I try to imagine the pre-burqa Kabul of the seventies, urbane, colorful, cosmopolitan. Women and men, dressing as they choose, saunter down tree-lined streets—no bomb-cratered avenues, no shell-riddled hovels—they speak freely to each other en route to work, to school, to homes that are painted, that have electricity and running water, windows and doors. No need yet for the Taliban to secure the area from rape and murder, no necessity yet for draconian measures to protect women and minorities from becoming the targets of renegade soldiers.

At the zoo we are met by the lion's keeper, a soft-spoken man named Sheraqa. Sheraqa Omar single-handedly saved the zoo from being closed down during the Taliban, and has since labored, without pay, to keep the handful of surviving—if malnourished— animals alive. He had to compile every reference to animals he could find in the Koran and present them to the Taliban's Ministry of Justice in order justify the zoo's existence. And with the war and shortages of food, those were tough times for the people of Kabul, let alone for a collection of starving animals. Hungry soldiers found them easy hunting, and bullies enjoyed their opportunity to torment a captive victim. They'd lure them with a promise of food, then jab them with sticks. Today, the brown bear's snout, or what's left of it, is still an open sore. But even before the Taliban, before Sheraqa inherited the zoo's forlorn survivors, the zoo suffered a continuing spate of sadistic soldiers. In the mid-nineties someone blasted the zoo's elephant with a rocket-propelled grenade, just for sport. Something about militarism and cruelty go hand in hand.

Sheraqa leads us behind the empty lion enclosure to an adjoining concrete shelter. He fumbles with the padlocked door and gestures for us to follow. At the length of a cold and narrow corridor is a chainlink stall, and beyond it a square of sunlight cut by the kennel's doorway. In that gold rectangle is a breathing thing, an immense font of breath, a sighing, fallen Jove. Sheraqa motions us forward. He opens the chainlink, and steps softly inside. The beast is startled awake and bolts to his feet, his head moving from left to right, listening for the intruders he can not see. "Mar-jan . . . Mar-jan," Sheraqa intones. He reaches out to touch the bony spine at the lion's hips. Marjan trembles at the touch, and shifts his weight. His remaining eye is crust-ringed and stunningly bright in its blindness. "Mar-jan," Sheraqa repeats, this time simply as another kind of caress. The lion knows his keeper well. He yawns and shows his gums, his exhalation like a wave that sweeps the room.

The translator tells us how years ago a cocky soldier, in an arrogant display of virility, jumped into Marjan's cage and was swiftly brought up short. The lion mauled the fool, then had his best meal in weeks. The next day the victim's brother returned, threw in a grenade and killed Marjan's mate. Marjan, blinded and bloodied, managed to live.

The beast licks his scar-puckered muzzle, shakes his mane, and stumbles lamely toward the kennel door, showing us the skeleton frame that, though racked by injury and malnutrition, held up through even old age.

"Taliban did that?" I ask, pointing to the caved-in skull and the one eye that somehow glows with its own light.

Sheraqa shakes his head no, and sighs with the resignation of someone who's seen every stripe of human savagery.

"Mujahedeen," he offers with flat philosophical candor. "Panjshiri."

At this moment in Kabul every sentry on the road is from Panjshir, every guard at every gate, every bureaucrat at every desk. They are the heroes of the hour, the securers of the interim peace. But this hardly feels like security to those who remember life in Kabul in the mid-nineties. Massoud's crowd stormed this neighborhood of west Kabul, killing thousands of Hazaras and razing the area in one of the city's most grisly sieges.

This afternoon there are, thankfully, no soldiers. The only thugs loitering at the zoo are young boys. They are dirty and seem Dickensian in their street-spun cruelty. Where, I wonder, do they live? They throw dirt and pebbles at the falcons and the owls, they taunt the monkeys, and yell insults at the brown bear, whose vulnerability they scorn. The worst in the bunch is a baldheaded kid, shaved probably to rid himself of lice, his revealed skull flecked with scars. He is himself a kind of exhibition piece, exemplary in his obvious rage. A friend wacks him on the head, then runs away, delighted with himself. The other boys laugh excitedly. For a reason I can't bear to imagine, these kids find thrill in provocation. They like to watch the seething. It strokes them.

On our way to the exit we pass our lion, now sprawled and breathing outside in the parched sunlight.

" . . . a shape with lion body and the head of a man,/ A gaze blank and pitiless as the sun."

I am thinking again of Yeats' *Second Coming*, his meditation on the moral center that cannot hold against cyclonic forces. . . .

" . . . while all about it/ Reel shadows of the indignant desert birds."

It could go that way here. . . . The peace may not hold.

On the other hand, I have the words of James Baldwin to sustain me.

"The world," he insisted, "is held together by the love of a few people." This pronouncement, childlike as it is, is true, I do believe;

and everywhere in Kabul, for every molecule of evil there appears to exist two of love.

We grasp the hands of the soft-spoken man, and look into his eyes, and bid him good-bye.

On the way home, the street markets glow with the light of a setting sun. We dodge wooden carts full of radishes, carrots, and cauliflower. This is what the much-feared site looks like: carts heaped with tangerines, almonds, and raisins. Donkeys and old men and laughing girls. Carpets and coats, firewood and mattresses.

This place is brutal, bruised and moldering. Yet it percolates, delights, extends its hands. Potatoes, chilies, red and yellow onions. . . .

"Did you see that?" Cilantro and cabbage, pumpkins and leeks . . . "Another woman without the burqa . . . that makes six so far, . . . " apples and lemons, petrol and baby clothes. . . .

Sometimes a woman's gaze will burn at you, even from underneath her blue hood, and her head will turn to follow yours, and you feel the stare is full of hope. If she is old she might already have her cheeks in the sun, and smile into your eyes, then continue to count her change.

Or a child will wave as if greeting a storybook creature. Or an old man will squint and cock his head as if he's recognized someone he hasn't seen in a long while.

"Hello, how are you?" they all shout into your window. Tea and musical instruments, plumbing fixtures and bicycle tires.

"I am fine!" you shout back, and my god, it's true.

Hanging legs of lamb, sheep heads, and sausages. Coils of fried pastries and stacks of flatbread. . . .

"How much for two lemons?" "How much for a scarf?"

"You like carpet?" "Come, lady, see my shop."

Cartons of juice, cigarettes, soaps. Pink Chinese toilet paper, radios, and cassettes.

They crowd you, they touch, but they don't push. We are all curious and tickled. And I stare back at them, because we're both amazed.

How is the site of devastation? What is the place of no "what ifs"?

"How are you?"

. . . Candlesticks and dead chickens. Kites and munitions. Tin drum heaters and Russian army boots. . . . "How are you?"

The place wants to live. It's patient, a green soul inside the seed.

If you stumble in the street, the urchin who regularly torments you is there at your elbow, helping you to stand. "Lady," she croons in her real voice, "Its OK."

. . . Replicas of French furniture . . . mufflers and tool sets . . . t-shirts, satellite dishes, wiper blades. . . .

The evening air is blue, cold and milky; there's a haze muting the scene, quelling the bluster. There aren't enough industries yet for the making of smog, and the diesel fumes from cars like Najib's can't match what you've left on the other side of the world. This soup is a combination of wood smoke and dust . . . product of the day's enterprise. By eight o'clock it's thick as a fog.

It might take a while for the veil to be lifted, before safety once again saunters under the shade. If James Baldwin and his love sustain us, it might just happen.

How and when does each know she'll be safe?

Rather than waiting for freedom to be granted, might we claim our safety and throw off our veils? When is it ever safe? How are we to know our freedom? From whom does power come?

The dust saturates my clothes, and it smells good, like clay and river rock, wood smoke and human sweat. When I get back to the States, it takes a few washings to get it out.

* * *

For months The Pile's genie continued to rise, an ongoing release of horrid energy. I breathed its fumes, and felt haunted.

I was working at the World Trade Center six days before the attack. I was spending real flesh-and-blood time at a place that is now atomized. I have my security badge from Tower One tacked to my bulletin board. I probably rubbed shoulders with the folks I later choked on. Everyone has her story of that morning, or of that building, or of the people who lost their lives.

So this is the new image, the picture that will contain all the narratives we are in the midst of discovering. The image is still coalescing in the facets of the event, an aggregate, more complex than any cinematic montage. It is more like a hologram, a wraith coming to us from the Future, some new form, at once mythic, plural, apocryphal, multidimensional; and inside it there is no distinction between Cain and his brother, between the towers, the planes and the ruin, between the toxic cloud and the glistening autumn in which it looms, between the survivors and The Pile.

But let's not leave it at that. On the day I journeyed down to Ground Zero someone had scrawled the message "God Bless This World" over and over across the windows of a jewelry store at Broadway and Cortlandt. Someone had also written "I Love You" over and over in English on the walls of the football stadium in Kabul, the place where, weekly, the Taliban performed its executions. The new image will confirm that there is no distinction between the dross at Ground Zero and the heap at the top of the Panjshir Valley, between the dust of lions and dust in which prayers are scrawled.

That morning as I roamed around the barricades, and tried to salvage images from The Pile, and hoped to rescue my bearings, hordes of workers were beginning to swarm, each outfitted with ID badges, many with briefcases, each with a determined look, ready to get on with life, en route to a destination. We, by which I now mean, all of us human beings, are making our way through the dust: our source, our home, our destination.

Permissions

ACKNOWLEDGMENTS

Special thanks to Leslie Belt, Shelly Mandell, Barbara Pepe, Jane Thurmond, and especially to my editor, Tina Pohlman.